HIKING ALBERTA'S SOUTHWEST

Joey Ambrosi

Sponsored by
Sierra Club of Western Canada
(Alberta Group)

Douglas & McIntyre
Vancouver/Toronto

Douglas & McIntyre Ltd., 1615 Venables Street, Vancouver, British Columbia V5L 2H1

Canadian Cataloguing in Publication Data

Ambrosi, Joseph Graham.
  Hiking Alberta's Southwest

"Sponsored by Sierra Club of Western Canada
  (Alberta Group)"
Bibliography: p.
ISBN 0–88894–426–8

  1. Hiking – Alberta – Guide-books. 2. Trails –
Alberta – Guide-books. 3. Alberta – Description
and travel – 1950– – Guide-books. I. Sierra
Club of Western Canada. Alberta Group. II. Title.
GV199.44.C22A44 1984   917.123'044   C84–091155–6

Cover photograph by Derek and Jane Abson, Photo/Graphics
All photographs by Joey Ambrosi unless otherwise credited.
Design by Rosamond Norbury
Printed and bound in Canada by D. W. Friesen & Sons Ltd.

CONTENTS

The Continental Divide rises above Rainy Ridge Lake.

Preface

Through a series of grants from the Employment Development Branch of Employment and Immigration Canada, the Sierra Club of Western Canada since 1980 has been running historic trails projects in Calgary which involved researching the history of southwest Alberta. The idea of a trail guide was brought to the forefront in 1982, and during the summers of 1982 and 1983 the field research was completed, with archival and background research completed in the spring of 1983.

The completion of this trail guide would not have been possible without the combined efforts of a great number of individuals. First and foremost is Pat Kariel, Conservation Chairman of the Sierra Club of Western Canada. In her capacity as project co-ordinator, Pat has been responsible not only for the initiation of the project but also for its continuity. Her interest in preserving our heritage provided the spark for the entire enterprise. Pat's tireless work in overseeing all aspects of the project has been an inspiration to everyone involved.

Hikers working on the crew in the summer of 1982 included Bonnie Bentley, Hilary-Anne Hamilton, Paul Heintzmann and Will Neilson; Linda Smith in Calgary was secretary-bookkeeper. In the spring of 1983, much of the background research on geology and history was completed under the competent pens of Tim Bradnam and Darlene West, with Morgan Price initiating the first stages of the cartography.

The bulk of the hiking was completed in the summer of 1983: the crew included Colleen Boyle, Brad Fuller, Audrey Gordon, Hilary-Anne Hamilton and Sherry Tompkins. Bonnie Bentley, Joel Coates and Will Neilson also hiked with the crew for the first two weeks of the summer, before heading to Rocky Mountain House to work on a Sierra Club historic trails project in that region. Linda Smith continued in the capacity of secretary-bookkeepr. Special thanks are due to numerous volunteers, in particular, members of the Skyline Hikers of Calgary, who aided our effort by hiking several trails in the Highwood. Field research was completed by mid-July, and was followed by the unenviable task of organizing and compiling the trail guide in a presentable form. Colleen Boyle, Brad Fuller, Audrey Gordon, Hilary-Anne Hamilton, Will Neilson, Sherry Tompkins and Darlene West all contributed greatly to this phase.

Others involved with the production of this guide include Virginia Edgington and Heather Semple (project managers, 1980 and 1981), Miles DeVries (field researcher, 1980), Moira Semple (secretary-bookkeeper, 1981), Murray Wolf (researcher and interviewer, 1981) and Lorain Lounsberry (historical researcher, 1982).

Thanks are also due to the Alberta Historical Resources Foundation for financial assistance and to its executive director, Trudy Cowan, who took a keen interest in the preservation of the province's historic trails.

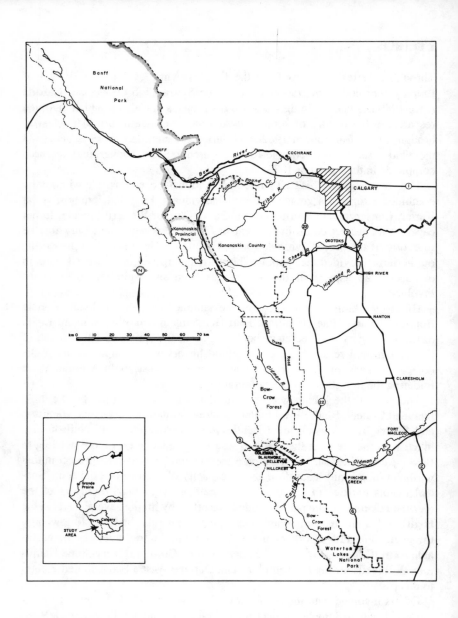

INTRODUCTORY NOTES

Perhaps the most striking feature of the landscape in Alberta's southwest corner is its variety, encompassing spectacular mountains, rugged foothills and dry prairie grasslands. Hikers exploring this region will follow dusty cattle trails, pass through abandoned mining towns and cross over scenic mountain passes. And like its landscape, this region's history is diverse—a legacy of explorers drawn to its wilderness and exploiters lured by its resources.

The story of southwestern Alberta's historical development and that of the trails are inseparable. Unlike the more established trails within the national parks, which offer hikers equally attractive opportunites for backcountry exploration, many of those in southwestern Alberta existed as bona fide routes only in the past. Although now easily accessible, they are largely unmarked and unmaintained.

The story of man's existence in this region endures today, where old pack trails surface in prairie grasses and along mountain streams. Some routes follow the paths of explorers; others were established in the course of everyday life.

Southwestern Alberta as approached in this guide is bordered on the north by the Bow River and on the south by the American border. Its easternmost boundary is Highway 2 south from Calgary and it stretches west across the foothills to the Continental Divide of the Rocky Mountains. It is a land blessed by nature with timber, mineral and petroleum resources, mountain-fed streams and winters modified by warm chinook winds.

Main access is provided by the east-west running Crowsnest Highway (Highway 3), which bisects the region. The Forestry Trunk Road, running north-south, divides the region north of Highway 3, as does the West Castle Road south of Highway 3. Both give direct access to the core of the hiking areas. Blairmore and Coleman are the main service centres for hikers; they offer gas, food and accommodation, and a number of outdoor specialty shops. A hospital and the Alberta Forest Service district headquarters are located in Blairmore. Pincher Creek, Claresholm, Nanton and Longview also provide services and facilities, as well as alternative access. Maintained forestry campsites are generously spread throughout the vicinity but there are also many primitive and unmaintained sites.

Hiking opportunites in southwestern Alberta are varied and rewarding. Even the most remote corners of the region can be reached with minimal effort. Long neglected as a prime hiking area, the Crowsnest backcountry receives few visitors and even the most accessible trails are little travelled, making this an area preferable to crowded national and provincial parks. Wildlife is abundant, and the secluded nature of the region makes each trip a true "wilderness experience." The majority of hikes are of the half-day or day variety, lending themselves well to family outings. Although overnight trips are few, the region does have plenty of routes that will challenge even the most seasoned backpacker.

Hiking in the area requires no special permits, although some hikes require permission from landowners, especially in the Porcupine Hills–Whaleback–Chain Lakes area, where much of the land is fenced for cattle grazing. *Be sure to check with landowners before setting out across private property.*

Geological History

The story of southwestern Alberta's past begins with the forces that shaped today's mountains and foothills. The diverse landforms defined the locations of early transportation routes: low mountain passes and river valleys were followed first by animals, then Indians, and finally by white men, and a network of trails was eventually established throughout the region.

The three main events in southwestern Alberta's geological history—the retreat and advance of ancient seas, the era of mountain building, and the era of glaciation—occurred over a period of thousands of millions of years. Figure 1 shows a chronology of the geological events of the last 2400 million years. During the earliest event, of which we know very little, seas advanced and retreated many times across western Canada. Evidence suggests that about 1600 million years ago seas moved eastward from the old Pacific Ocean across basement rocks and deposited thick layers of sediment. The mountains and plains of present-day Alberta are the result of many cycles of deposition and erosion. The prehistoric seas retreated from Alberta for the last time between about 105 and 67 million years ago.

During the era of mountain building, about 57 million years ago, the horizontal layers of sedimentary rocks that are now the Rocky Mountains were subjected to long and continuous compression. Under these high-pressure, high-temperature conditions, many rocks became relatively pliable and were folded into wavelike structures. Faults were created when some rocks broke or fractured and slid along surfaces of separation. Different types of folds and faults are visible today throughout the mountains and foothills of southwestern Alberta.

On the plains east of the Porcupine Hills, sedimentary rocks are relatively flat lying. To the west the foothills, which parallel the main ranges on a northwest-southeast alignment, are a belt of folded and faulted beds composed of Mesozoic sandstone, shale, conglomerate and coal.

At the Front Ranges, great sections of older sedimentary rocks have been moved substantial distances to the east or northeast along a number of low-angle thrust-faults. The major rock types are limestone, dolomite, sandstone and siltstone, usually of Paleozoic age, about 240 to 600 million years old. In a number of places older rocks have been moved many kilometres eastward

Fig. 1:

GEOLOGIC COLUMN AND TIME SCALE

ERA	PERIOD	EPOCH	SIGNIFICANT LIFE EVENT	MILLION YEARS AGO
CENOZOIC	QUATERNARY	RECENT		
		PLEISTOCENE	RISE OF MAN	
		PLIOCENE	ABUNDANCE AND GREAT VARIETY OF MAMMALS	
		MIOCENE		
	TERTIARY	OLIGOCENE	RISE OF MAMMALS	
		EOCENE	FIRST HORSES	
		PALEOCENE		65
MESOZOIC	CRETACEOUS		LAST DINOSAURS AND AMMONITES FIRST FLOWERING PLANTS	
	JURASSIC		FIRST BIRDS AND MAMMALS ABUNDANT AMMONITES	
	TRIASSIC		FIRST DINOSAURS	225
PALEOZOIC	PERMIAN		FIRST CONIFERS, LAST TRILOBITES MANY INVERTEBRATES DIE OUT	
	PENNSYLVANIAN		ABUNDANT SWAMPS – COAL INSECTS, AMPHIBIANS	
	MISSISSIPPIAN		FIRST REPTILES	
	DEVONIAN		FIRST TREES AND AMPHIBIANS ABUNDANCE OF FISH	
	SILURIAN		FIRST LAND PLANTS, CORAL REEFS	
	ORDOVICIAN		FIRST FISH	
	CAMBRIAN		MANY TRILOBITES	570
PRECAMBRIAN	UPPER PROTEROZOIC		PRIMITIVE INVERTEBRATES	
	MIDDLE PROTEROZOIC		SPONGES, WORMS, ALGAE, BACTERIA	
	LOWER PROTEROZOIC			2400
	ARCHEOZOIC			

and thrust over younger formations. In the Waterton Lakes National Park area, the Lewis Thrust, a major thrust-fault in the Front Ranges, roughly defines the base of the mountains.

For tens of millions of years before the onset of glaciation, gradational forces such as running water, wind and gravity eroded the new mountains and hills. Preglacial streams and rivers also eroded, transported and deposited material. When glacial ice first began to cover the area about two million years ago, the major rivers in southwestern Alberta—the Kananaskis, Elbow, Sheep, Highwood, Livingstone, Oldman, Crowsnest, Carbondale and Castle—were probably in approximately the same positions as they are today.

Glaciers, which form when winter snowfall exceeds summer melt, played a major role in the shaping of the landscape of southwestern Alberta. During the Ice Age—the Pleistocene era—glacial ice invaded all the valleys of the Rocky Mountains and foothills one or more times. As far as geologists can tell, there were at least four major ice advances in southwestern Alberta, the most recent ending high in the mountains between 6000 and 7000 years ago.

The ice age left its scars: a wide variety of landforms associated with glaciation are visible today. (Figure 2) The majority are the result of erosion; others are depositional structures.

9

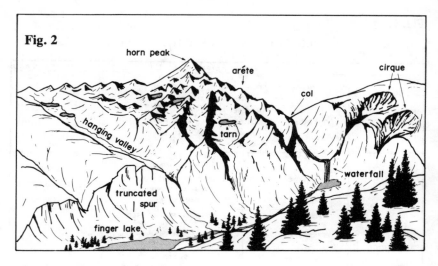

Fig. 2

horn peak
aréte
cirque
col
hanging valley
tarn
waterfall
truncated spur
finger lake

As the ice moved it scraped and scoured the land like a giant bulldozer. Preglacial soils and rock debris were carried along the bottom of glaciers. When the ice melted it deposited this material as till, which ranges in size from fine rock debris to boulders the size of a house. Mounds of glacial till are referred to as moraines.

Ice moving down pre-existing valleys had a tendency to straighten and widen them. Stream-cut valleys have a V-shaped appearance, whereas those that have been glaciated are more U-shaped. In some instances the main valley underwent more extensive glaciation than one of its tributaries. When the ice melted, the tributary was left hanging hundreds of metres above the main valley. This glacial formation is aptly called a hanging valley.

Cirques occurred where alpine glaciers originating high in the mountains scraped into the mountain face, giving it a bowl-shaped appearance. Sometimes a cirque contains a small lake, or tarn, which has been dammed by glacial debris.

One interesting phenomenon, also the result of glaciation, is a string of pinkish or purplish quartzite boulders, known as the Foothills Erratics Train, which stretches from a point southeast of Jasper National Park to an area beyond the international border. These rocks roughly parallel the mountains and are of a different material from the underlying bedrock. It is believed that during the Pleistocene, a landslide deposited tonnes of rock material onto a glacier in the Athabasca Valley, which then carried the debris southward and left it in a 650-km long line of irregular width. The largest of these erratics is Big Rock, located west of Okotoks.

Other landforms in the area associated with glaciation include drumlins, eskers, coulees, stream terraces, outwash plains and glacial spills. Today there are only a few remnant valley glaciers, but running water, wind and gravity continue to wear the mountains and plains.

Early Indian Life

The Great Plains—a vast grassy expanse with lush vegetation and buffalo in abundance—a hunter's paradise: this was the very heart of the North American continent some 7000 to 9000 years ago. Nomadic hunters drifted across the plains in small groups, preying on mammoth beasts. As the climate grew warmer, the ice sheets around Hudson Bay began to retreat. Rivers shrank and hunters were forced into the moister eastern and northern woodlands. By A.D. 1200, the Great Plains were largely devoid of men.

When the drought finally ended, living conditions improved along the rivers that flowed through the plains, and in Alberta, both climate and landscape became similar to what they are today. Moose, caribou and deer flourished in the forests of central and northern Alberta, and buffalo thrived in the select environment of the southern prairies. Over the centuries the buffalo multiplied on the prairie, and Indians once again settled on the ideal hunting grounds.

The Athapaskans, including the Cree Indians, inhabited the forest regions north of the North Saskatchewan River. The Sioux stock—the Assiniboines— migrating westward, occupied the lower Battle River Valley.

The Algonkians—the Bloods, Piegans and Siksikah of the Blackfoot Confederacy—once lived in the forests east of Lesser Slave Lake. They made the transition from small hunting and trapping bands to the larger groups necessary for the buffalo hunt, and pushed south and west in the quest for better hunting grounds, ultimately holding most of the immense territory extending from the North Saskatchewan River to the southern headwaters of the Missouri, and from longitude 105° west to the base of the Rocky Mountains. Despite their forest origins, they adapted quickly to plains culture.

The Kootenay initially dwelt east of the Rocky Mountains, ranging on the Great Plains as far east as Saskatchewan. (The name Kootenay is a corrupted form—possibly by way of the Siksikah language—of Kutonaqa, one of the Kootenay's names for themselves.) However, they were eventually forced off the plains by the Blackfoot. Indian territorial boundaries were not well defined; they changed frequently as the more aggressive tribes wrested land from the weaker ones.

By the mid-eighteenth century, the southwestern Alberta area was Blackfoot country. (Although there is some dispute over the origin of the name Blackfoot, it is believed to refer to the discolouring of the natives' moccasins by the ashes of prairie fires.) The Blackfoot dwelled in tipis and shifted regularly from place to place following the buffalo herds. The hunt demanded manpower; since it was usually undertaken in warm weather, the carcasses had to be skinned and the meat at once placed on drying racks to prevent it from spoiling.

A restless, aggressive and predatory people, the Blackfoot were constantly at war with neighbouring tribes, and their hostile character discouraged travel by white men. A trader described the Blackfoot as "the most powerful nation we are acquainted with. War is more familiar to them than to other nations. . . . In their inroads into the enemies' country they frequently bring off a number of horses, which is their principal inducement in going to war."

The arrival of horses from the southwest in the mid-eighteenth century provided a new mobility for Plains Indians and threw them into contact with other tribes. Enemies three to five hundred kilometres away were now within raiding distance; the prairie was becoming smaller. Horse-stealing raids inevitably provoked counterattacks and with the added stimulus of guns, war took its place alongside the buffalo hunt as a focal point of Plains Indian life.

The Kootenay had by this time been forced west of the mountains by the Blackfoot. Their buffalo hunting expeditions regularly brought them back to the plains, and conflicts with the Blackfoot, who knew the mountain passes almost as well as the Kootenay, continued. To avoid bloody confrontations, increasingly difficult passes came into use, until the Continental Divide ranges were netted with trails.

Like the Blackfoot, the Kootenay were nomadic, nonagricultural people. In addition to the plains buffalo, they hunted deer, elk, moose and bear in the valleys of the Columbia and Kootenay rivers. Salmon, found in abundance at the head of the Columbia during the fall spawning season, became an important part of the Kootenay's diet.

The most recent arrivals to the foothills region are the Mountain Assiniboines, or Stoneys. (The name Stoney comes from their custom of cooking meat in holes with water heated by hot stones.) Originally a branch of the Assiniboines of Manitoba and North Dakota, they were a plains tribe and member of the Sioux nation. Diseases such as smallpox, syphillis and measles, along with Blackfoot warfare, drastically reduced their numbers, and the tribe eventually split, with one portion migrating south and west to the region of present-day Montana. Another small band continued slowly westward, settling in the foothills near modern-day Morley in the early nineteenth century. These Stoneys remained culturally tied to the plains, but occasionally they ventured across the mountains to the valleys of the Columbia. They became familiar with the eastern foothills of the Rockies and developed extensive trail networks.

Other Indian tribes, including the Sarcee to the north, the Cree to the east, and the Gros Ventre and Nez Percé to the south, made brief forays into the region for trade or plunder but never established any lasting territorial claims.

The Explorers

When the first explorers ventured into what is now Alberta, it was part of the Hudson's Bay Company's immense empire. These adventurers were in search of valuable furs found in abundance in northern forests.

Although there were fewer fur-bearing animals in the south, the Hudson's Bay Company recognized the importance of establishing a southern pass through the Rockies—a route to link existing trading posts with the Pacific. Also, American settlers were moving into the Oregon Territory (modern-day Washington and Oregon). A southern pass would facilitate British settlement west of the mountains and thus substantiate Britain's claim to Oregon. But long after northern passes had become virtual highways in the wilderness, the threat of Blackfoot attack continued to discourage travel in the south.

Southern Alberta was considered perilous territory. In 1834, the Hudson's Bay Company's Bow Fort (also known as Peigan Post), located above the Bow River near its junction with the Kananaskis, was abandoned. During its short existence as much time was spent fighting with the Blackfoot as trading with them. Several employees lost their lives defending the fort, and when the last traders had fled, Indians burned the buildings to the ground.

Peter Fidler, a company employee, was the first explorer to pass through the southern region. He crossed and mapped the Battle, Red Deer, Bow and Highwood rivers and was the first surveyor to map the exact course of much of the North and South Saskatchewan rivers. In the early nineteenth century other company employees had passed through the territory, but no crossings of the mountains were recorded.

It was inevitable, though, that this territory would be penetrated by white men. The danger and adventure of travel in the south—and probably the prestige associated with crossing an unknown path—appealed to pompous men like Sir George Simpson, Governor-in-Chief of the Hudson's Bay Company, who was known as "The Little Emperor." He accomplished the first recorded crossing of a southern route through the Rockies in 1841 as part of an incredible round-the-world journey. Viewed by some of his contemporaries as arrogant and unpredictable, Simpson was notorious for making excessive demands on his travelling companions, while seldom suffering any discomfort himself. Pushing his party to its limits, he demanded long days in the saddle, and allowed few rests. Simpson's cavalcade of forty-five horses, guided by Peechee, a Cree chief, crossed the prairie at a rapid pace, and even through the rugged mountains they covered an incredible forty miles per day.

Simpson and his party entered the Rockies at Devil's Gap and Lake Minnewanka. They reached the Bow River and presumably followed an old Indian trail to the head of Healy Creek, a tributary of the Bow, crossing the Great Divide over what is known today as Simpson Pass.

In June 1841, a party of over one hundred settlers set out across the prairie from Fort Garry with the hope of reaching Oregon before winter. Their leader was James Sinclair, a Red River half-breed. In a day when only the boldest ventured into Blackfoot country, Sinclair's slow-moving Red River cart train rambled over prairie and foothills, with men, women, children, cattle, horses and dogs. Awaiting the party at Fort Edmonton were Simpson's instructions for them to cross the mountains via Athabasca Pass, the Hudson's Bay

Company's regular route of travel. But Sinclair was determined to find his own crossing.

In direct defiance of Simpson's orders, the party headed south toward present-day Canmore and crossed White Man Pass, which until then had been known only to Indians. The Red River emigrants finally arrived at Fort Vancouver after almost five months of travel. They were rewarded only with disappointment, for they encountered difficulty securing the land they had been promised from the Hudson's Bay Company.

Sinclair himself returned to the Red River and ventured west on two subsequent trips for the company. In 1854, he led another party of Red River emigrants through the mountains to Oregon. This group, along with 250 head of cattle, followed Simpson's route but traversed the Rockies at Kananaskis Pass. (Kananaskis is a corruption of Kin-e-ah-kis, the name of a Cree brave who, according to legend, had a miraculous recovery from the blow of an axe.) Because of inhospitable terrain, the Red River carts that had been serviceable on the prairies had to be abandoned just past the site of Old Bow Fort and a pack train organized. Three feet of snow made the pass treacherous, but the party arrived at Fort Walla Walla, in present-day Washington, with a minimal loss of stock.

James Sinclair settled at Fort Walla Walla in 1855, but was prevented from establishing a viable business because of persistent Indian problems in the Oregon Territory. Indian hostility continued into 1856 and in March of that year Sinclair was killed in an Indian attack at the Cascades on the Columbia River.

Although the Hudson's Bay Company was responsible for much of the early traffic on the trails, some travellers were on religious missions. Among them was the rotund, black-robed Jesuit missionary Father Pierre-Jean DeSmet who, in 1845, made his way eastward to the prairies to settle an uprising among the Blackfoot. He, too, crossed the Continental Divide at White Man Pass and, near a small lake at the summit of the Divide, erected a cross. DeSmet prayed that his "Cross of Peace" might be "a sign of peace and salvation to all the scattered and itinerant tribes east and west of these gigantic and lurid mountains." The stream DeSmet followed to the summit is now called the Cross River.

In 1845, the possibility of open conflict between Britain and the United States over the Oregon Territory loomed large. Capt. Henry J. Warre and Lt. Mervin Vavasour were sent on a secret mission by the British army to find a possible route for troops to Oregon. The pair were disguised as "private individuals seeking amusements" and likely followed the same route Sinclair had taken four years earlier. They concluded that the steep and rocky mountain passes would not be suitable for the passage of troops. Britain never did send troops to Oregon and the conflict was peacefully resolved in 1846 by a treaty extending the 49th parallel to the Pacific.

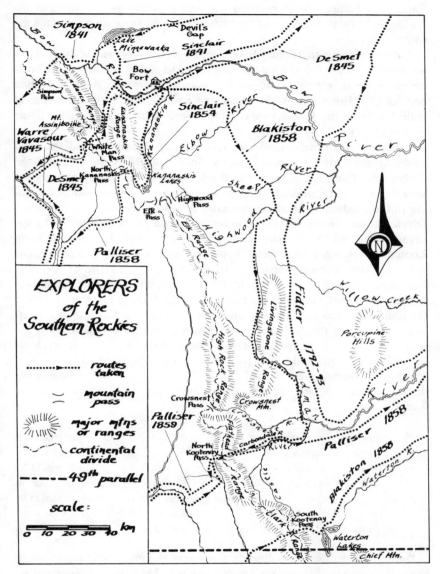

EXPLORERS of the Southern Rockies

········▸ routes taken

︶ mountain pass

╲╲╲╲╲ major mtns or ranges

╲╴╲ continental divide

──── 49th parallel

scale:

0 10 20 30 40 km

As for DeSmet, he succeeded in pacifying the Blackfoot and returned to the Columbia River via Athabasca Pass in the spring of 1846. Having been warned by the locals that he was too heavy to attempt such an arduous journey, the missionary fasted for thirty days prior to departure.

The potential for profitable activity other than fur trading in southwestern Alberta was probably not given serious consideration until after the Palliser expedition of the 1850s. Backed by the British government and organized by

Capt. John Palliser, the expedition was sent to determine the value of the prairie for farming, mining and lumbering and to find new routes through the southern Rockies.

Palliser, along with Thomas Blakiston, Eugene Bourgeau and James Hector, explored the prairies, Kananaskis, Crowsnest and Waterton regions. Hector, a geologist, naturalist and medical doctor, discovered Bow, Vermilion and Kicking Horse passes. Bourgeau, an amiable and dedicated botanical collector, spent much of the expedition's duration in the Bow Valley doing botanical work.

Blakiston, a magnetic observer, was sent by Palliser to find the most southerly route within British territory. In August 1858, he ascended the Carbondale River, referring to it as the Railway River because of the great advantages he felt it offered for a railway entry into the mountains. Continuing to the headwaters of the Carbondale, Blakiston reached the Continental Divide at North Kootenay Pass, descended to the Flathead River and journeyed to the Elk River. His return trip in 1858 took him across South Kootenay Pass, which he named "Boundary Pass," claiming it to be the most southerly pass in British territory. He was obviously unaware of Akamina Pass, ten miles farther south, and still three miles north of the 49th parallel.

Captain Palliser's explorations took him up the Kananaskis River valley to the Kananaskis Lakes, following the route of James Sinclair's 1854 expedition. He crossed the divide at North Kananaskis Pass and descended the westward-flowing river that still bears his name. At the Kootenay River, local Indians told him that Blakiston's party had passed by five days earlier.

Palliser's journals made special note of the difficulty of travel through the dense forests, a hazard encountered by every party that had crossed the Rockies:

> The obstacle which a burnt forest presents to the traveller is of all the others the most arduous; sometimes we were in a network of trees, lying at all angles the one to the other, and requiring no small amount of skill to choose which should be removed first. It was extraordinary to observe the great care taken by our horses in extricating their feet and legs from dangerous places. The poor brutes seemed to be very expert at this kind of work, and even when caught they would evince the utmost patience, and free themselves as gently as possible.

During the Palliser expedition's three-year duration, a comprehensive report on conditions in the West was compiled. The group encountered no hostility from the Blackfoot, and reported abundant arable and favourable mining prospects. It was inevitable, therefore, that the next arrivals were entrepreneurs.

Settlement and Development

Among the first profit-seekers to arrive in southwestern Alberta were the whiskey traders. Predominantly American-based, they were a wild and daring lot who used whiskey, or more often their own potent concoctions, to secure buffalo robes from the Indians. In the 1870s the whiskey trade was flourishing on the prairies, with devastating effects on the native people. The Indians traded buffalo robes for whiskey, blankets and trinkets. They were dying of white man's diseases, in fights and drunken brawls, and—now that the buffalo were all but gone—of starvation.

In 1873, the Indians' plight prompted the newly formed Dominion Government of Canada to recruit the North West Mounted Police force. The journey the following year by some 275 members of the NWMP from Fort Dufferin, Manitoba, to the foothills of the Rocky Mountains—the almost 900-mile "March West"—is undoubtedly the most celebrated event in the force's history.

In addition to curbing the illicit whiskey trade, the police provided security, opening the way for settlement in the west. In the late 1870s, shortly after the establishment of Fort Macleod, a NWMP post was established in the Crowsnest Pass at Police Flats (Passburg). This post was later abandoned in favour of stations at Pincher Creek and Frank.

Ranching was the first major industry in the foothills of southwestern Alberta. American and eastern Canadian cattlemen and British financial backers were attracted to the dry climate and mountain-fed rivers for raising livestock. The Canadian government provided a strong incentive through an order-in-council which allowed one man or one company to lease up to 100 000 acres of grazing land at the rate of one cent per acre per year. Duty was removed on cattle that were brought into the country and allowed to mature and multiply for a minimum of three years.

By 1884, the ranching industry was well established, with most of the activity centred in the foothills south and west of Calgary; there were forty-one ranch companies holding leases totalling 2 782 000 acres (1 126 000 hectares). Although the ranchers enjoyed a profitable era, their industry was not without problems. There were struggles between absentee landowners, who had little knowledge of the business, and ranch managers. Disease, wolves, prairie fires, theft and harsh winters took their toll on cattle numbers. Settlers were now arriving in ever-increasing numbers from the east and from Europe. The same government that had advocated large-scale ranching was now, through legislation, opening the country to homesteaders, and the heyday of the giant cattle ranches was coming to a close.

The lumber industry, spurred by the growing demand for building materials as migrants flowed westward, soon followed ranching. In 1880, the federal government set up a sawmill south of Crowsnest Pass on Mill Creek. The following year the mill was purchased by Senator Peter McLaren, a lumber magnate from Perth, Ontario. McLaren's mills in the Crowsnest grew rapidly, supplying ties for the CPR's transcontinental line.

The region's immense potential in lumber and coal was realized by the earliest visitors. However, most came in search of that ever so elusive mineral, gold. Although no fortunes were ever made, legends of the mother lode, in the form of the Lost Lemon Mine, remain embedded in local folklore. Its existence has never been proved, but many locals claim that it lies in wait somewhere deep in the High Rock Range.

While the gold boom proved to be a bust, prospectors noted the abundance of coal in the Crowsnest. Entrepreneurs called for a rail line to link Crowsnest coal and newly discovered lead/zinc/silver deposits at Kimberley with the Trail-Rossland smelter complex. Initial surveys were completed in 1892, but financial difficulties prevented the Crowsnest Pass Railway from becoming a reality until 1898.

Begun in 1897, the line was pushed to within 19 km of the Crowsnest Pass summit by year's end. The labour force on the rail line fluctuated between 1500 and 4000; a considerable number were Chinese who had worked on the CPR mainline through the mountains. The rail line was completed in the fall of 1898, and opened the Crowsnest to civilization. The coal mining boom was quick to follow, and within a few years towns sprang up all along the railway—Burmis, Passburg, Bellevue, Hillcrest, Frank, Blairmore, Coleman, Sentinel and Crowsnest. Immigrants, largely from Europe, poured in to work the mines. Some of the towns were short-lived, but others prospered and survived to become the very heart of the region today.

In the past two decades, the oil and gas industry, despite a slow start, has grown steadily and now stands alongside coal and lumber as one of the key industries in the Crowsnest. Tourism also supports the local economy, for the region is blessed with an abundance of natural beauty.

Climate

The climate of southwestern Alberta is generally described as cold continental, with long, cold winters and short, cool summers having brief hot spells. Precipitation peaks in the summer and thunderstorms occur regularly. Summer hikers must be prepared for prolonged cold, rainy periods when the temperature occasionally falls below freezing. Rapid weather changes emphasize the need for adequate reserve clothing, even on hot, sunny days. Temperature also varies greatly with altitude, generally decreasing 2°C for every 300 m of altitude. Snowfall can occur in the high country in any month, and early autumn storms often deposit up to 20 cm any time after mid-August. Such accumulations usually melt quickly, though, and September and October often provide fine hiking weather.

Although described as long and cold, winters in the Crowsnest are moderated by regular chinook winds, which keep winter snow accumulations at a minimum in valley bottoms. Moist air masses from the Pacific deposit precipitation across British Columbia, crossing the Continental Divide and descending into Alberta as warm, dry winds. Temperatures can change rapidly with onset of a chinook, often rising 20°C in a few hours. The prominent "chinook arch" appears as a bright band of sky below a dark grey cloud across the western horizon.

Accumulations of snow are greatest at the Continental Divide, lessening to the east. The lower foothills of the Rockies and areas such as Porcupine Hills are generally free of snow by early May, allowing ideal early season hiking. Generally speaking, trails below 1600 m are free of snow by early May; trails between 1600 m and 2100 m open between mid-May and early June, and trails over 2100 m usually open by late June. These rough guidelines are modified by a number of factors, including proximity to the Continental Divide (greater winter snowfall at the divide); facing of slope (snow lasts longer on north- and east-facing slopes); and seasonal snowfalls (heavy or light winter snowfalls will greatly affect early season hiking). Any combination of these factors can cause fluctuations in the hiking season of four to six weeks.

Vegetation

In southwestern Alberta, vegetation is extremely diverse and varies within relatively small areas. The most noticeable feature is zonation—that is, changes in vegetation at higher altitudes. Four major vegetation regions are represented here: the predominant Boreal Forest, the Montane Forest, the Subalpine Forest, and the Alpine.

The Boreal Forest region covers the foothills of the Rocky Mountains and the lower elevations of the Front Ranges. Here the distinctive tree species is the lodgepole pine; trembling aspen and balsam poplar are also abundant. This combination is the first to grow back after a forest fire, and remains dominant until the slower growing spruce take over and the short-lived pine and aspen fall down or die out. In older forest stands, white spruce is common.

The lodgepole pine (18 to 30 m tall) is a slender, straight tree that grows in dense stands. The cones are small, allowing lodgepole pine to regenerate quickly and dominate recently burned areas. They remain on the tree many years, but open soon after the intense heat of forest fires.

The trembling aspen (12 to 18 m tall) has a long, cylindrical trunk and a short, rounded crown. Its leaves are nearly circular and have an abrupt short, sharp tip; they tremble in the slightest breeze.

The white spruce (24 to 36 m tall) has a uniform conical crown with branches that spread or drop and extend slightly to the ground. Its 2-cm-long needles are stiff with blunt ends. The cones of the white spruce have smooth tips, while the tips of the cone scales on the Englemann spruce are toothed, notched, or pointed.

The balsam poplar (18 to 25 m tall) has a long, straight, cylindrical trunk with a narrow open crown of a few stout, ascending branches. Its leaves are 8 to 13 cm long and are egg-shaped, gradually tapering to a sharp tip.

The Montane Forest is present in many of the region's river valleys. This forest is primarily a mixture of Douglas-fir and lodgepole pine. Limber pine, white spruce, Englemann spruce and trembling aspen often overlap there.

The Douglas-fir (45 to 60 m tall) has a long, branch-free cylindrical trunk and a short, flat-topped crown. The young trees are very attractive, with a narrow conical shape that extends to the ground. The needles are 2 to 3 cm long and are often sharply pointed.

The limber pine (8 to 18 m tall), named for its flexible young branches, grows in rocky, exposed places. Mature trees have short trunks that are usually crooked and irregularly limbed. They also have a large, uneven crown. The 8-cm-long needles are crowded in bundles of five.

In the drier lower elevations of the Montane Forest, vegetation consists of trembling aspen groves and grasslands, mixed with rose, saskatoon, junipers and occasionally white spruce. Willows and other shrubs grow at moist, less well-drained sites, such as near creeks and rivers.

The Subalpine Forest occurs at higher elevations on the eastern slopes of the Rocky Mountains. The distinguishing vegetation is the Englemann spruce–white spruce hybrid, replaced at higher altitudes by pure Englemann spruce. Lodgepole pine is the fire-successional species, but subalpine fir is more common at higher elevations. At lower elevations, whitebark pine is found along with the hybrid spruce and lodgepole pine. On exposed ridges and above the tree line, limber pine and some whitebark pine and subalpine larch are present.

The Englemann spruce (18 to 35 m tall) has a crown that is generally symmetrical, narrow and spire-like. Because it is tolerant of shade it may have branches extending over nearly its whole length, especially in open stands and on steep hillsides. Its needles are 2 cm long and its cones are cylindrical to narrowly oval, 3 to 8 cm long.

The subalpine fir (20 to 30 m tall) is often dwarfed at the timber line (2 to 5 m tall). Its needles are deep blue-green, flat, blunt and upcurved. The cones are dark and, as with all firs, erect. The cone scales fall separately, leaving the "candle" standing on the tree.

The whitebark pine usually has a short, rapidly tapering trunk and wide-spreading crown. When exposed to strong winds, it is often reduced to shrub-size, with widespreading irregular and twisted branches that lie almost flat on the ground. This pine seldom grows more than 12 m high, but in favourable conditions can sometimes reach 25 m. The cones are distinct from those of other pines, being egg-shaped to almost globular.

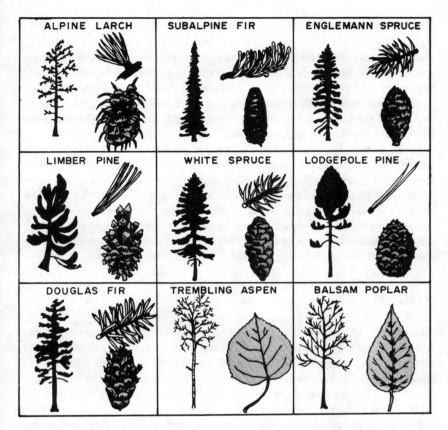

ALPINE LARCH	SUBALPINE FIR	ENGLEMANN SPRUCE
LIMBER PINE	WHITE SPRUCE	LODGEPOLE PINE
DOUGLAS FIR	TREMBLING ASPEN	BALSAM POPLAR

The subalpine larch grows to a height of 18 m. It has a short, sturdy trunk that tapers rapidly into a ragged-looking crown of irregular branches and clusters of many deciduous needles growing from short shoots. Its cones are 5 cm long and have pointed bracts between the scales. The larch's needles turn to a beautiful golden colour in the autumn before falling off for the winter.

The highest vegetation zone is the alpine. Resembling the rolling tundra of the arctic in its lower reaches, the Alpine zone supports a plant cover of shrub, willows, grasses, sedges, heaths and forbs. The growing season seldom exceeds sixty days, and strong winds gust at speeds averaging three times greater than in the valleys. During the brief flowering season, generally from late July to August, alpine meadows are knee-deep with many species of colourful flowers, while the more exposed, higher and windier slopes abound with miniatures of flowers—2 to 5 cm in height instead of their normal 15 cm or more—common at lower elevations.

Flowers

The Crowsnest area is endowed with a great assortment of wildflowers. Many species follow the receding snowline in earliest spring, while others do not appear until the heat of midsummer. As a general rule, later summer sees the final blooms, and usually indicates the arrival of autumn in the high country. Because of the large number of species in the area, wildflower enthusiasts are advised to carry a guidebook with them.

In the foothills grassland, hikers will likely encounter prairie crocus, asters and purple fringe. In the higher, forested regions, flowers such as Indian paintbrush, calypso orchid, columbine and purple virgin's bower are more prominent. In alpine meadows, the glacier lily, forget-me-not, white globe flower, fleabane and purple saxifrage are common. Frequently, flowers are not unique to one zone: some such as cinquefoil, arnica and mountain heather are scattered between alpine and forest regions, and others such as shooting star and wild rose are found in both the forest and foothill zones.

Animals

Encounters with wildlife are regular occurences when hiking in southwestern Alberta. The area is home to a wide variety of animals, ranging from the minute shrew, weighing only about 5 gm, to the imposing bull moose, standing from 1.5 m to over 2 m at the shoulder and weighing up to 800 kg. Some animals, such as cougars and grizzly bears, are very rare and are seldom seen by hikers.

Of the larger animals inhabiting southwestern Alberta, members of the deer family are the most frequently sighted. The largest is the moose, whose range extends from forested mountain valleys out onto the foothills. Generally solitary animals, moose are often seen in marshy or open, logged-out areas where they feed on the tender young vegetation. A cow moose protecting her calf, or an enraged bull, can be a formidable opponent, and as with all wild animals, hikers should keep their distance.

Elk, or wapiti, occupy much the same range as moose. Large animals, weighing up to 360 kg, they are distinguishable from other deer by their sheer size, as well as the white rump patch and dark neck. A mature bull elk's antlers are a majestic sight, measuring up to a metre long. Travelling in herds, elk inhabit all of the forest zones of the region, migrating to higher elevations for the summer and returning to valley bottoms in winter.

Two species of deer, the white-tail and the mule deer, are found in all the region's vegetation zones. The mule deer is the larger of the two—a mature male weighs up to 180 kg—and is distinguished from the white-tail by a number of physical features. The mule deer has a large white rump patch and distinctive "mule" ears. Antlers also differ, the mule deer's being forked

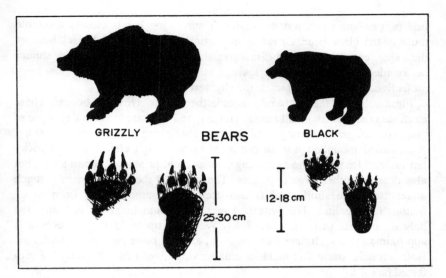

GRIZZLY   BEARS   BLACK

25-30 cm

12-18 cm

while the white-tail's have several tines growing from a single branch. White-tail deer, weighing up to 150 kg, are noted for the bushy white underside of their tail, which waves like a white signal flag when the animal is alerted and flees. Both species live in forested valleys, with large herds of mule deer found in the vicinity of Whaleback Ridge and Porcupine Hills.

Rocky Mountain bighorn sheep, especially mature males, may weigh up to 150 kg. They live in large herds at high elevations in the summer, wandering along ridge tops and alpine meadows, then migrate to the protection of valley bottoms in winter. Grey-brown in color, bighorns possess distinctive curved horns and white rumps. Table Mountain supports a herd of 200 or more, attracted to the area by a natural salt lick on the south flank of the mountain.

A shy and seldom seen ungulate is the mountain goat. This shaggy, white animal with short, black horns can weigh up to 140 kg. Mountain goats have a very limited habitat, dwelling on high, rocky terrain where they are safe from most predators.

Of the many carnivores inhabiting this corner of Alberta, probably the best known and most feared is the bear. Two species live here, the black and the grizzly. The black bear, much more common than the grizzly, is found throughout the region. Contrary to its name, it comes in assorted hues, from cinnamon to brown and even tan. These bears can weigh up to 225 kg but average about 150 kg. They are omnivorous and spend much of their time eating berries, roots, grass, insects and small rodents. Carrion (dead and decaying animals) also makes up a small portion of the black bear's diet.

Grizzlies are larger and more unpredictable in their behaviour than black bears; their average weight is about 300 kg although weights up to 450 kg have been recorded. They seldom venture down into the valleys, usually staying at high elevations, and prefer open avalanche slopes where they can find berries and catch rodents easily. Their eating habits closely resemble those of the black bear. Grizzlies are distinguishable from the black bear by their size, concave face and distinctive shoulder hump. Both species should be avoided, especially in the spring, as new cubs can make a sow very protective, and she will attack at the slightest provocation.

Flesh-eaters of the cat family include the cougar, lynx and bobcat. These cautious creatures avoid all human contact, and it is rare to catch a glimpse of one. The cougar is the largest of the three, weighing in the range of 100 kg. Also called mountain lion or puma, it favours high elevations and rocky terrain, and frequents the same ranges as its prey, principally small game, but also deer and other large ungulates. The lynx and the bobcat are very much alike; they have similar habits and occupy the same regions from valley bottom to tree line. The lynx is larger, paler and longer-haired than the bobcat, and has distinctive ear tufts. Weighing up to 13 kg, the bobcat is approximately 3 kg lighter than the lynx, and has more prominent markings. Both animals' basic diet includes small rodents, with rabbits being the preferred fare.

The coyote is the most common member of the dog family in the region, and is spread throughout all vegetation zones. Seen most regularly in open grasslands along the foothills, it feeds on small rodents and is a major factor in controlling their populations. Another common member of the dog family is the red fox, which, being naturally cautious, is not often sighted. Although the fox feeds largely on field mice, rabbits and insects, fruit and berries also make up part of its diet. Wolves are reported to inhabit remote mountain valleys, but they are extremely rare.

Among the small mammals commonly seen, the beaver is one of the most noticeable. Numerous small dams and ponds attest to much beaver activity. Almost every valley has its resident beaver family, and hikers will undoubtedly walk past a dam and lodge, and if fortunate may even catch glimpses of beavers at work.

Weighing up to 10 kg, the porcupine, with its unmistakable spiny coat and distinct waddle, is often sighted on trails. Since it has an annoying habit of chewing anything salty, hikers must be careful to keep packs, boots and clothing away from this pesky creature.

Both pika and marmot live in the extremely limited environment of rocky alpine terrain. The marmot is renowned for its shrill, piercing whistle which accounts for its French name of "siffleur" or whistler. Often seen sunning themselves on rocks, marmots are inquisitive by nature, and seldom run unless closely approached. Much more wary and elusive is the diminutive pika, or "rock rabbit," weighing only 100 g, who shares alpine rock slopes with the marmot and can usually be seen scurrying between rocks. Affectionately known as "hay farmers," pikas collect grass and dry it in the sun before storing it for the winter.

Rabbits are a common sight in southwestern Alberta. The dominant species is the snowshoe, or varying hare. Named for its ability to change colour with the season, the varying hare goes from dark brown in summer to white in winter. It is also known as the snowshoe hare because of its large feet, which become very furry in winter, giving good traction on the snow. Predators include cougar, lynx, bobcat, fox and coyote.

Squirrels and chipmunks are the most frequently seen small mammals. Although they are accomplished moochers, they should not be fed, since they can become dependent on humans for food and then fail to find and store enough natural food to survive the winter. Red squirrels, with their rusty fur and bushy tails, can be glimpsed running around the treetops and jumping from tree to tree, descending to the ground for food. Their constant chatter quickly reveals their presence.

The two common species of groundsquirrels are the Columbian and the golden-mantled. The Columbian has the widest range, usually from around 200 m to 2450 m elevation. Although its overall colour is buff, the back is dappled black and tan. The golden-mantled groundsquirrel is rarely found lower than 1500 m, and prefers sunny forests with an abundance of fallen logs. Its name is derived from the golden-brown mantle covering its head, neck and shoulders. Each side has two broad, whitish lateral stripes, bordered by narrow, black ones, running from the shoulder to the rump. Because of these stripes, it is easily mistaken for a chipmunk. But the most common species of chipmunk—the least chipmunk—is not only smaller but has black and white stripes which reach to the eyes.

Other mammals inhabiting the area include minks, martens, weasels, wolverines, bats, skunks, badgers, lemmings, muskrats, pack rats and a great variety of mice. Frogs and toads are the most common reptiles in the wetter portions of the region, though alligator lizards, garter snakes and bull snakes are also sighted from time to time.

Birds

Many birds, including hawks, owls and ducks, inhabit southernwestern Alberta, or pass through during yearly migrations. The number of species are too numerous to mention in detail, and budding ornithologists are advised to take along a bird guide. Some more common species, however, are regularly seen on hikes.

In the foothills, Porcupine Hills and Whaleback Ridge areas, the ruffed grouse, prairie chicken, red-tailed hawk and saw-whet owl are occasionally seen by sharp-eyed hikers. More common are the yellow-bellied sapsucker, least fly catcher, mountain bluebird, mourning dove and three-toed woodpecker, as well as Cassin's finch and lazuli bunting, both of which are at the northeastern limit of their range.

The forested region of southwestern Alberta is home to many species. The pesky Canada jay and Clark's nutcracker, along with vociferous crows and ravens, are often found scavaging around campsites. Some of the more common species are warblers, sparrows, finches, chickadees, vireos and nuthatches. Being on the edge of the great northern flyway, the Crowsnest Pass region plays host to a great number of migratory species from spring through fall.

Ptarmigan, horned larks, grey-crowned rosy finches and fox sparrows are regular companions to hikers above the tree line. Occasionally, golden eagles and bald eagles will be seen circling overhead, guarding alpine environs.

Hiking

The terrain in southwestern Alberta is comprised of grassy foothills, forested valleys, alpine meadows and rugged mountains. There are no glaciers in this area. Trails run the full gamut from bushwhacking to game trails, hiking trails and outfitters' horse trails to seismic lines, four-wheel-drive roads and abandoned logging roads. Since none of these is located in any provincial or national parks, few are maintained. With the logging, mining and oil industries still very active in the region, the condition of many of the trails is constantly changing.

Trails have been categorized as follows:

Half-day hike: can be completed in an afternoon, requiring no more than 4 to 5 hours of hiking time (including return).

Full-day hike: can be completed easily in a full day, requiring no more than 8 to 10 hours return.

Backpack: will require more than one complete day of travel.

Easy: running shoes will suffice; trail well defined, no major elevation gain.

Moderate: minor fords; trail may become difficult to follow; topographic map recommended; notable elevation gain.

Difficult: major fords; bushwhacking, scrambling; topographic map essential; major elevation gain.

For a typical day hike in southwestern Alberta a suggested equipment list would include:

Essentials

day pack
sturdy boots and wool socks
warm clothes
rain gear
hat
sun-glasses

first aid/survival kit
flashlight
topographic map
compass
food, canteen with water
insect repellent
sunscreen

Optional, but recommended

  camera, extra film
  binoculars
  nature guide books

This list is by no means complete, and you may wish to add items where necessary.

Backpacking

Non-impact camping cannot be overemphasized. The back-country environment is fragile and easily destroyed, and care must be taken to preserve it. Now that there are more people on the trails, it is up to all of us to ensure that we enter, visit and leave the area in a clean and natural state.

To prevent the depletion of natural firewood, we recommend using gas stoves when backpacking. If you are staying two or more nights at the same campsite, move your tent each night. Besides giving you variety, this protects the vegetation beneath your tent. Dig your toilet away from water sources and your camp; burn toilet paper and cover toilet when you leave. Keep your campsite clean and free of food. Pack out garbage; leave nothing behind to cause problems with bears and other wildlife.

Hazards

As in all mountain areas, southwestern Alberta has natural hazards. The natural environment can be a killer of the unprepared, but a severe injury or loss of life can be avoided if precautions are taken. Know your physical limitations. If you are not properly trained or equipped to climb, don't attempt that 60 m cliff that blocks your path. If a river is swollen with spring runoff and there's a strong possibility of getting swept downstream, turn around and come back another day. If a sudden midsummer snow storm erupts, plummeting temperatures below freezing, and your group is outfitted with shorts and T-shirts, head for home.

Mountain climates vary: a warm, sunny morning can easily change into a cold, snowy afternoon. It is important to take a few basic precautions, so that your hikes remain safe and relaxing.

Be aware of rapid weather changes. Carry warm clothing and rain gear. Remember that as you go higher in elevation, the temperature falls. Be sure to allow enough hiking time to get back to your car before nightfall. And remember that topographic map and compass are essential. Maps are available at Alberta Forest Service Offices located throughout Alberta.

Hypothermia:

Hypothermia occurs when the body temperature falls below normal. Hypothermia can attack anyone, and can occur even in temperatures well above freezing. Death can occur within two hours of the first symptoms. It is extremely important to know causes, symptoms and treatment.

A few safeguards can be taken to avoid hypothermia. To prevent extreme heat loss, dress properly, and protect your body from the cold, the wet and the wind. Susceptibility is greater if you do not eat properly, sleep properly or control muscular activity to avoid perspiration. Alcohol and tobacco also hinder the body's adjustment to cold: alcohol causes blood vessels to dilate, while tobacco causes them to constrict, which can decrease skin temperature.

River Crossings:

River crossings are a potential hazard of the area. The following precautions are recommended. Wear running shoes to aid traction, and use a staff for extra balance and support. Unfasten your hip belt for easy removal of your pack in case of a fall. When crossing, keep in mind that logs and stones can be slippery. Do not underestimate the speed of shallow water, and stand sideways to the current for best balance. Even when confronting a narrow creek, it is often advisable to ford, as a long jump with a heavy pack can easily result in an injury.

Bears:

Bears and other wildlife are inevitably encountered during backcountry travel. As with most wild animals, bears are very unpredictable. There are no ways to prevent bear encounters and confrontations, only precautions.

Be alert at all times in the backcountry. Make your presence known, either by using bear bells or by talking. Pets are best left at home, as they can incite a bear attack; so can the smell of perfumes and cosmetics. Be especially cautious around streams, where sounds are drowned out, or near prime feeding grounds such as avalanche slopes and berry patches. Avoid a direct confrontation with a bear. Make a wide berth around a black bear, and totally avoid a grizzly, even it it means turning back.

If caught in a confrontation, do not antagonize the animal. Be aware of the presence of cubs, as a sow will be overly protective and may attack. Stay calm and assess the situation. There is no absolute solution. Remember that you cannot outrun a bear. Options include climbing a tree or playing dead, the latter requiring much nerve on behalf of the hiker.

Backpacking in bear country requires bear-proofing your campsite. Hang food out of reach of bears, at least 50 m from your tent site. Never leave food around your camp, and be sure to pack out all your garbage.

Ticks and Bees:

Ticks and bees are two pests to be aware of. Ticks are known to carry Rocky Mountain Spotted Fever, which can be fatal if not treated in its early stages. A bee sting can also be fatal if the victim is strongly allergic.

Wood ticks are most prevalent in the early season, up to six weeks after snows have melted. As a precaution against them, tuck pants into socks when hiking and if at all possible avoid brushing the undergrowth. Check yourself thoroughly at the end of each day, as ticks can usually be found before they have had time to penetrate. If a tick has penetrated, pull gently and steadily with your fingers, but avoid pulling so hard that the head breaks off and remains embedded. Other options for removing ticks are to suffocate them using gasoline or vaseline, or to apply a source of heat, such as an extinguished match. Clean area thoroughly after a bite. Remember that an imbedded tick, or part of one, requires medical attention if you can't remove it yourself. Bee stings are inevitable: be prepared. Carry antihistamines in a first aid kit to reduce swelling. Hikers aware of a bee allergy should always carry a bee sting kit. Hikers unsure of their allergic reaction should check with a doctor before heading into the backcountry.

Hunting Season:

Autumn is hunting season in southwestern Alberta, which creates another hazard for hikers. Almost the entire region is open to hunting, and with the amount of big game available, hunters will be found everywhere. Although the majority of hunters are responsible and cautious, there will always be the exception who prefers to "shoot first and ask questions later." If hiking during this season, be sure to wear bright colours and make your presence known. Also be on the watch for carrion (decaying animal remains) from a hunter's kill—it attracts bears that may become overly protective of this food supply and can attack without provocation.

Maps

Maps reproduced in this book do not replace topographical maps but are for orientation only. The following legend is common to most of these maps.

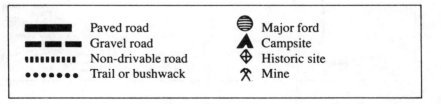

▬▬▬	Paved road	⊜	Major ford
▬ ▬ ▬	Gravel road	▲	Campsite
ⅢⅢⅢ	Non-drivable road	⊕	Historic site
●●●●●●	Trail or bushwack	人	Mine

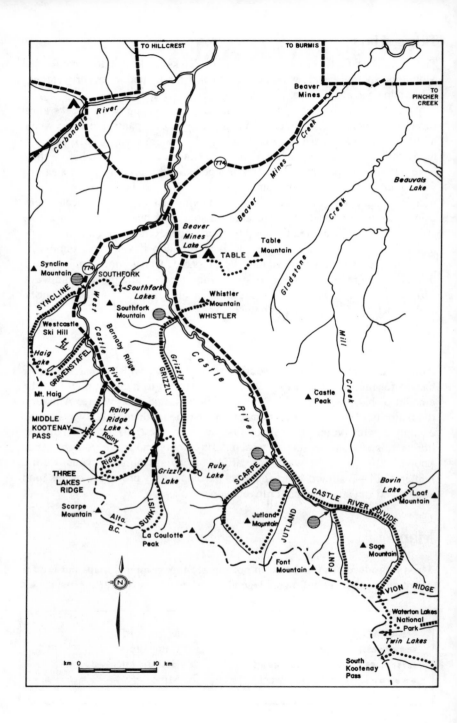

CASTLE RIVER AREA

Castle Peak, standing 2555 m high, and located along Windsor Ridge, lends its name to the major river in the area. The Castle River and its tributaries generally flow from south to north as the Continental Divide turns eastward and approaches the Waterton Lakes National Park boundary. The Carbondale River, Mill Creek and Beaver Mines Creek are the major tributaries entering the Castle River before it turns east and flows into the Oldman River southeast of Cowley. The valleys of the Castle and the West Castle rivers are low and long, extending far up into the Clark Range. Alpine glaciers carved the valleys into their present U-shape, leaving behind hanging valleys and truncated spurs.

Many forest fires occurred throughout Alberta during the dry spells of the 1930s. A furious fire storm in 1936 burned tens of thousands of hectares of mountain timber, and today, extensive stands of 40- to 50-year-old lodgepole pine and widespread charred snags testify to the extent of that burn.

Forestry campsites in the area include Beaver Mines Lake and Castle Falls, which may be reached from Highway 774.

Grizzly Lake seen from Grizzly Creek Trail

FONT CREEK (Sage Mountain Loop)

Day hike/backpack; difficult
Length: 19 km (11.4 m) round trip
Hiking time: 8 to 11 hours
Elevation gain: 550 m (1800 ft.)
Maximum elevation: 2180 m (6900 ft.)
Map: Sage Creek 82 G/1
Access: Drive to the end of (South) Castle River Road, 20 km south of the Castle River bridge. The road is impassable beyond this point. Hike south on remains of the road (washed out in sections). The route up Font Creek is 5 km south of the trailhead.

This long but interesting circuit of Sage Mountain begins by a steady climb up Font Creek valley, the crossing of a low ridge and a steep descent to the headwaters of the Castle River. The remainder of the loop follows the banks of the river, eventually returning to the trailhead. After 5 km of road walking, the real hike begins at the junction of Castle River Road and Font Creek Road where the Castle River (15 m wide, thigh deep) is forded. Take the left (upper) fork 2.5 km up Font Creek. There are two waterfalls to the west on the ascent of Font Creek valley. After a final steep pitch, the trail reaches a saddle at the 7.5-km mark. From the ridge, Waterton Lakes National Park, Avion Ridge and Anderson Peak are visible to the south.

The descent from the ridge is very steep, and sturdy boots are recommended. At the headwaters of the Castle River, old logging roads swing around Sage Mountain, eventually completing the circuit. There are a limited number of sites where camp can be set up in Font Creek valley and upper Castle River areas.

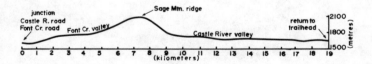

BOVIN LAKE

Day hike/backpack; moderate
Length: 11 km (7 mi.) to lake
Hiking time: 7 to 8 hours return
Elevation gain: 520 m (1700 ft.)
Maximum elevation: 2040 m (6700 ft.)
Maps: Sage Creek 82 G/1; Beaver Mines 82 G/8
Access: Drive to the end of (South) Castle River Road, 20 km south of the Castle River bridge. The road is impassable beyond this point. The route to Bovin Lake continues south on remains of the road, which is washed out in sections.

Set in a rocky basin, the clear blue waters of the lake are a welcome sight at the end of a long, hot day. Splendid views of the prairies, Waterton Lakes National Park and the Clark Ranges along the Alberta–British Columbia boundary make the steep climb up and over the ridge to the lake well worth the energy.

Starting at the end of a maintained road, the trail is a four-wheel-drive road heading south down the Castle River valley. Within the first 400 m of the trail there is a washout on Castle River. Keep to the left bank of the river to avoid a major ford here and at the next junction of trail and river.

From here the trail heads south down the valley, offering good views of Avion Ridge on the north border of Waterton Lakes National Park. Approximately 5 km from the trailhead the trail cuts up to the left, following a seismic line. The next 4 km are a tedious uphill climb through an enclosed forest, with views opening up of the Castle River valley as elevation is gained.

The trail continues around the east side of the mountain to the saddle of the ridge. From here the trail is obvious as it descends into the basin and continues east. Keep left at an intersection to Bovin Lake approximately 400 m farther on. There are adequate campsites along the lakeshore.

Extra time can be spent climbing the ridges on either side of the saddle, where the view is even more extensive.

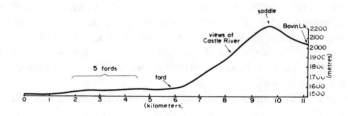

33

SCARPE CREEK

Day hike; difficult
Length: 8.2 km (5 mi.) to end of trail; 9 km (5.5 mi.) to top of ridge
Hiking time: 3 to 5 hours to top of ridge
Elevation gain: 365 m (1200 ft.) to end of trail; 700 m (2300 ft.) to top of ridge
Maximum elevation: 860 m (6100 ft.) to end of trail; 2195 m (7200 ft.) to top of ridge
Map: Sage Creek 82 G/1
Access: The route begins on the west side of (South) Castle River Road, aproximately 20 km from the Castle River bridge. The road ends 200 m past Scarpe Creek access and is in fair condition as far as the access. To find the trailhead, follow the road down to the bank of the Castle River. A road begins on the opposite side of the river, just north of the Scarpe Creek/ Castle River confluence.

The trail follows an old road up Scarpe Creek valley, eventually reaching a small basin at the valley's head. Three subalpine lakes can be reached with a moderate amount of bushwhacking. An option is a ridge walk to Lys Ridge and Grizzly Creek valley. Alternate trails also exist at the head of Scarpe Creek valley via high cols to Sage Creek (British Columbia) and to Jutland Brook. The Jutland Brook option is a loop trip, ending at the Scarpe Creek access on the Castle River Road. The hike up Scarpe Creek offers solitude, frequent wildlife, and some fine valley scenery, with the ridge between Scarpe and Jutland creeks giving outstanding views in all directions.

As you approach the Castle River, notice some outfitters' corrals. Ford the river (difficult, 20 m wide, thigh to waist deep, fast flowing) and make your way along the west bank through marsh and willows. You eventually reach a road on the north bank of Scarpe Creek. Travel is easy here as the road passes through a lodgepole pine forest. As the road rises, Mount Coulotte is prominent directly ahead, and Mount Jutland is seen to the south. Ford Scarpe Creek three times (10 m wide, knee deep), watching for the occasional fallen log to cross on. After the third ford, the road swings south around the flank of Mount Jutland. LaCoulotte Ridge parallels the trail, guarding the west side of the valley. Across the valley several fine tributary waterfalls tumble down from LaCoulotte Ridge. The road soon ends, and gives way to a single-file trail, which continues on the semi-open slope of Mount Jutland, on the east side of the creek. Near the end of the valley, the low pass to the right (west) leads to Sage Creek in British Columbia. No trail exists across the pass, though the route is obvious.

The trail ends in a small basin near the source of Scarpe Creek. From the trail's end, there are good views back down the creek to LaCoulotte Ridge,

Mount Coulotte and Lys Ridge. The route to Jutland Brook is up to the left (east); it leads over an open burned slope to a small rock outcrop above the basin. The route is very steep, rising nearly 350 m in 0.8 km, but the views from the ridge make the climb well worth the effort.

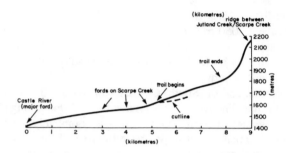

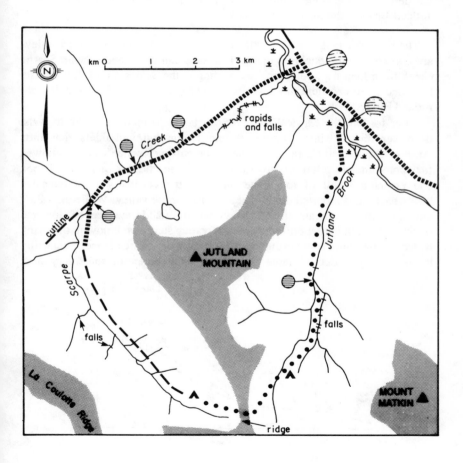

JUTLAND BROOK

Day hike; difficult
Length: 5 km (3.1 mi.) plus 1.5 km (1 mi.) of road walking
Hiking time: 3 to 5 hours
Elevation gain: 535 m (1750 ft.)
Maximum elevation: 2050 m (6700 ft.)
Map: Sage Creek 82 G/1
Note: There is no easy route to the basin at the head of Jutland Brook. Much bushwhacking will be required.
Access: Drive to the end of (South) Castle River Road, 20 km south of the Castle River bridge. The road is impassable beyond this point. Hike on the road for approximately 1.5 km. (One section is completely washed out.) After crossing the open gravel slope above the river, head west and ford Castle River. A cut-line begins on the west side of the river, north of Jutland Brook's confluence with the Castle.

The bushwhacking route up Jutland Brook leads through a secluded valley, always close to the bubbling creek. The route can be combined with Scarpe Creek for a loop trip, beginning and ending at the Scarpe Creek access. The loop makes an excellent day hike, with outstanding views from the Scarpe-Jutland Ridge.

After fording the Castle River (very difficult 20 m wide, thigh to waist deep, very fast flowing), find the cut-line, overgrown with alders, that starts north of the Jutland/Castle confluence. The cut-line, which can be followed for approximately 1 km, climbs steeply up the north bank of Jutland Brook and enters a forest of lodgepole pine. At the cut-line's end, extensive bushwhacking is required up the steep Jutland Brook valley. While the valley undergrowth is moderate, there is heavy windfall, and travel can be slow and tedious. Remain on the north bank as the valley steepens, enjoying the many waterfalls that tumble down Jutland Brook along its entire course. Eventually the terrain levels out at a large fairly open basin containing some very large

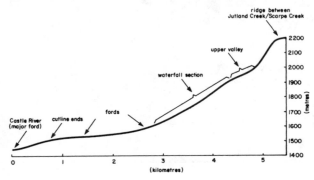

36

white spruce as well as alpine firs and Englemann spruce. From the basin, the gap to Scarpe Creek is up loose scree to the right (west).

If you have the time and energy, the ridge separating Scarpe Creek and Jutland Brook is an excellent hiking option, with a panoramic view extending for many miles in all directions. Kishinena and Akamina ridges and the mountains of Waterton Lakes National Park stand out to the south, Commerce Peak and Langemarck Mountain to the southwest, and Font Mountain and Mount Martin to the east.

GRIZZLY CREEK

Backpack; difficult
Length: 10 km (6.2 mi.) to Grizzly Lake
Hiking time: 4 to 6 hours one way
Elevation gain: 520 m (1700 ft.)
Maximum elevation: 2000 m (6600 ft.)
Maps: Beaver Mines 82 G/8; Sage Creek 82 G/1
Access: There are two possible access routes to the trailhead. The simplest is to ford the Castle River near its confluence with Grizzly Creek, but this is only practical at low water levels in late summer. To reach the ford, drive south on Castle River Road, turning off just before the Beaver Mines Lake Campground, and continue south for approximately 10 km. The road down to the ford is just past the road up to the Whistler Mountain Fire Lookout. To avoid the ford, bushwhack about 5 km along the west bank of the Castle and then pick up the Grizzly Creek trail where it descends to the ford. The alternate access is just across the Castle River bridge on West Castle River Road. Here, various lumber roads and overgrown trails roughly parallel the river, but the going is tedious.

Despite the difficult access, this trail provides a satisfying overnight hike up an isolated, high-walled valley to a pair of secluded lakes nestled between sheer rock cliffs. Small Ruby Lake and larger Grizzly Lake can remain ice-covered into early summer. Ruby Lake borders on the alpine vegetation zone, the light green bands of larch near the shoreline contrasting with the darker rock above.

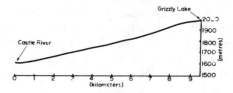

The road from the ford enters the gap between Lys and Barnaby ridges and gains some elevation, crossing and recrossing the creek several times before following a cut-line high along the east side of the valley. Near the beginning, several old cut-lines intersect the trail, but the main route is obvious. From the head of the valley, an optional route leads up to Lys and Barnaby ridges.

GRIZZLY LAKE (West Castle River Access)

This option for proficient scramblers and route-finders can reduce the time and distance to reach Grizzly Lake. Be forewarned that this route involves 400 m of elevation in the first kilometre and has no defined trail over its entire route. A topographic map is essential. Do not attempt this route in foul weather, since the slopes up Barnaby Ridge from the West Castle River are extremely hazardous when wet.

Beginning at the bridge, 6.5 km south of the West Castle Ski Area, make your way along skid roads and avalanche slopes to the scree and rock slopes of Barnaby Ridge, directly east of the road. From here it is a matter of ascending the most likely looking gulley to the ridge above. Watch out for falling rock. When you reach the ridge, where there are numerous game trails, continue south. Keep to the crest as much as possible, although even here some bushwhacking and scrambling will be required. (If any problems arise, bushwhack due east to the horse trail along Grizzly Creek.) Two km from where the ridge walk began, Grizzly Lake becomes visible in the valley below. Eventually you reach a well-worn trail that leads through loose scree to the southwest corner of the lake.

WHISTLER MOUNTAIN LOOKOUT

Half-day hike; moderate to difficult
Length: 2.6 km (1.6 mi.)
Hiking time: 1½ to 2½ hours to lookout
Elevation gain: 730 m (2400 ft.)
Maximum elevation: 2160 m (7100 ft.)
Map: Beaver Mines 82 G/8
Note: Carry drinking water, as there are no rivers or creeks along the way.
Access: Take Beaver Mines Lake Road towards the campground and follow the first road to the right to Castle River Road. Continue on this road for almost 5.5 km, keeping your eyes open for the trailhead on the left, which is difficult to see if you are not watching for it. It is marked by a short telephone pole that is no longer in use. If you come to a road that turns off to the right you have missed the trailhead.

This trail maintains a steady uphill grade for much of the distance, with occasional very steep sections. The large elevation gain in a short distance makes for strenuous work, but the excellent views from the summit are rewarding. Some of the recognizable mountains include Castle Peak, Mount Gladstone, Barnaby Ridge, Windsor Ridge, Lys Ridge, Table Mountain and the Flathead Range. From the summit, there is an almost aerial view of the meandering Castle River and its tributaries.

The trail passes through a forest of lodgepole pines for a short distance, then, after the first switchback, opens onto an exposed hillside. This hike is a paradise for botanists and wildflower enthusiasts, as a large variety of wildflowers, including such rare species as the trillium, bloom on the exposed hill in early summer. Take along a wildflower guide. The open slope provides good views of the nearby mountains and valleys. Barnaby Ridge is in constant view from the trail, guarding the west side of the Castle River valley.

The footpath fades away before the summit is reached, but the final climb is easy. At the top of this peak are the foundations of old fire lookout buildings. Built in 1966, Whistler Lookout was abandoned in 1975 by the Alberta Forest Service because the location was too windy and did not provide a view of a large enough area for fire control.

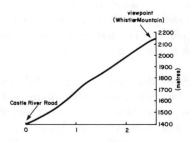

TABLE MOUNTAIN

Half-day hike; moderate
Length: 8 km (5 mi.) round trip
Hiking time: 2 to 3 hours to summit
Elevation gain: 765 m (2500 ft.)
Maximum elevation: 2225 m (7300 ft.)
Map: Beaver Mines 82 G/8
Access: The signed trailhead located in the Beaver Mines Lake Campground is found approximately 500 m past a bridge near the campground entrance on the right side of the road.

Table Mountain is a short hike to the top of a striking geological formation, with excellent views of the surrounding area.

Approximately 500 m past the trailhead, pass through a gate and follow alongside a small creek in a forest of trembling aspen and subalpine fir. There are several forks on this part of the trail. Always take the left fork; the right forks lead down to the creek. Much of the lodgepole pine forest in the area has been destroyed by pine beetle infestation; the many diseased "red" trees are visible from most viewpoints.

The trail emerges onto benches above the tree line on Table Mountain. Watch for mountain sheep, which are attracted to a natural salt lick on the south side of the mountain. The last leg of the climb is up the back of the mountain on a scree slope. Use caution here to avoid starting small rock slides.

At the summit, enjoy the panorama: peaceful Beaver Mines Lake lies almost 880 m below the north face of Table Mountain and directly to the west is Barnaby Ridge. Windsor Ridge, Castle Peak and Windsor Mountain are visible to the south, and to the west, the impressive peaks of the Flathead Range guard Alberta's border, while to the north the Porcupine Hills stand out in the distance.

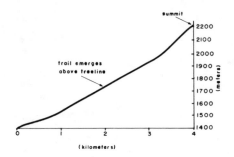

SUNKIST RIDGE

Day hike; moderate
Length: 6.3 km (4 mi.) to top of ridge
Hiking time: 2½ to 3½ hours
Elevation gain: 730 m (2400 ft.)
Maximum elevation: 2285 m (7500 ft.)
Map: Sage Creek 82 G/1
Access: Drive 12 km south of the West Castle Ski Area on West Castle River Road. Park at the fork in the road, which is in poor condition beyond this point. The route follows the fork to the left.

The north end of Sunkist Ridge, dividing the watersheds of the upper West Castle River and Commerce Creek, is situated on the Alberta–British Columbia border, and makes for a scenic day hike. The route is very steep in sections, rising over 500 m in the final 4 km. From the ridge an option exists to continue down the rough road along Commerce Creek for some 15 km, eventually reaching the Flathead River.

The first 2 km of the hike pass through areas extensively scarred by logging activity. At the 3-km mark, ford a minor tributary of the West Castle River. Immediately after the ford there is a large clearing, and the road becomes difficult to follow. Continue south and pick up the route on the far side of the clearing. The trail winds its way up the valley, the grade increasing as the road enters an enclosed forest. Approximately 1 km into the forest, take the fork to the right and continue to climb steadily. The forest cover opens along the side of a long steep ridge.

Because this is an east-facing slope, snow remains in the upper section into early summer, and travel can be difficult. There are fine views back down the West Castle valley: far below, a small lake nestled among the trees indicates the source of the West Castle River. At the crest of the ridge is the interprovincial boundary. Commerce Peak stands a mere 5 km southwest, and impressive Langemarck Mountain rises prominently in the south. Commerce Creek valley lies directly below, and the rough track can be followed down to the valley bottom.

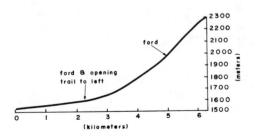

THREE LAKES RIDGE

Half-day hike; easy to moderate
Length: 4.3 km (2.6 mi.) to first lake
Hiking time: 3 hours
Elevation gain: 455 m (1500 ft.)
Maximum elevation: 2000 m (6600 ft.)
Map: Sage Creek 82 G/1
Access: Drive 10 km south from the West Castle Ski Area on West Castle River Road. The road forks here: take the left fork to the trailhead which begins 750 m farther, on the right-hand side of the road.

Picturesque subalpine lakes and their surroundings are a highlight of this hike below peaks of the Continental Divide. The trail begins along a logging road leading north and west around the base of Scarpe Mountain. At the 1.5-km mark, the road crosses the creek, but no bridges exist today. Instead, you must ford the creek or cross on one of the many fallen trees which span the creek downstream. The road becomes less defined as it leaves the creek, cutting across berry patches and leading up the north side of the valley. Along the somewhat steep ascent, ford the outlet from the first lake. At the valley head, a short scramble over the low ridge to the right (north) leads to the lake, surrounded by fir and spruce trees and juniper bushes. Bears and deer are regular visitors, and you may even catch a rare glimpse of a blue jay near the lakeshore. To the east are good views of the West Castle River valley, Lys Ridge, Jutland Mountain and Three Lakes Ridge.

For the adventurous hiker, a 200-m-high scramble over the next ridge will lead to the second lake. Be forewarned that this route is for explorers only, as no trails exist, and the scramble presents a formidable challenge. The third lake, to the south, is not easily reached from this route. However, another small lake to the north, on the British Columbia side of Rainy Ridge, is accessible to those with route-finding and mountaineering experience.

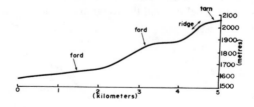

RAINY RIDGE LAKE

Rainy Ridge Lake, stocked with rare golden trout, is an exquisite gem of an alpine lake. Set beneath the sheer cliffs of Rainy Ridge, it is one of the most pleasant spots in the Castle River region. But routes to the lake are long and difficult and a topographic map is essential. One alternative route begins at the lakes on Three Lakes Ridge and leads north in the general direction of Rainy Ridge Lake on a rough and ill-defined trail. The trail remains well above the valley floor, passing immediately beneath several cliff bands before rising above one final cliff and swinging west into the Rainy Ridge Lake basin. Once in the basin, the trail becomes more distinct as it follows the south bank of the outlet creek, eventually reaching the lakeshore. A volunteer fisherman report and hiker registration box will be found at the shore, and several suitable campsites are situated at the east end of the lake.

The second option is much shorter, at least in terms of distance, but requires a great deal of heavy bushwhacking and a very good sense of direction. Using a topographic map, begin on the West Castle River Road directly east of Rainy Ridge Lake. When you reach the outlet creek, cross and continue up along the north bank. With a bit of scouting, an easy ascent route can be found in spite of one mossy cliff bank. Vegetation thins towards the upper basin. Continue along the banks of the creek until you reach the lake. Note: Although the distance is only a few kilometres on the map, you can expect to bushwhack for 3 to 5 hours to reach the lake.

Mountains northwest of Middle Kootenay Pass

MIDDLE KOOTENAY PASS

Half-day hike; easy
Length: 2 km (1.3 mi.) to pass
Hiking time: 1 to 1½ hours to pass
Elevation gain: 260 m (850 ft.)
Maximum elevation: 1950 m (6500 ft.)
Map: Beaver Mines 82 G/8

Access: Follow West Castle River Road to the West Castle Ski Area, turning left immediately before the ski area parking lot. Cross the West Castle River bridge and follow the gravel road for approximately 2.6 km. Take the right fork and cross the river once again. The road is driveable for approximately 3 km and heads uphill in the direction of Middle Kootenay Pass. The driveable section ends abruptly at a large ditch. Park here and hike on the road beyond the barrier. En route to the pass, keep an eye open for a natural sulphur spring on the west bank, 0.3 km downstream of the West Castle River from the last bridge.

Used by Kootenay Indians as a route across the mountains, Middle Kootenay Pass is a pleasant hike to a striking subalpine pass. From here, several options exist: continue down Middlepass Creek into British Columbia; take a ridge walk from the pass onto Rainy Ridge; or enjoy an easy scramble up a small peak to the northwest.

From the trailhead, Rainy Ridge dominates the south flank of the pass while distinctive Syncline Mountain and the pyramidal form of Mount Haig stand out to the north. The road now heads steadily uphill through a large, open logged-out area. In the early season, snowbanks remain on the road from this point on. Ford a small tributary that crosses the road. The road loops south through a burned-out area where many snags remain. Englemann spruce are prominent along the trail.

Although the elevation here is only 1900 m, the terrain appears almost alpine, for little regeneration has occurred since the major forest fires of the 1930s and the area has a stark, almost lifeless appearance. However, quite the opposite is true as wildflowers abound in the immediate vicinity of the pass.

From this vantage point, you can gaze far down Middlepass Creek into British Columbia. To the north are Syncline Mountain, Carbondale Hill and the Livingstone Range, while Barnaby Ridge dominates the view to the east. For excellent vistas of the Middle Kootenay Pass environs, ascend the small summit immediately northwest of the pass.

GRAVENSTAFEL BROOK–HAIG LAKE

Half-day hike; easy to moderate
Length: 3.5 km (2 mi.) to Haig Lake
Hiking time: 1 to 1½ hours to end of trail
Elevation gain: 400 m (1300 ft.)
Maximum elevation: 1800 m (5900 ft.)
Map: Beaver Mines 82 G/8
Access: Follow West Castle River Road to the West Castle Ski Area. The trailhead is at the south end of the parking lot.

This short, very steep climb leads up from the West Castle valley to a cirque beneath the heights of Mount Haig and Gravenstafel Ridge where grey rock cliffs are reflected in quiet Haig Lake. Scattered clumps of gnarled pine and fir accentuate the alpine character of this hanging valley.

To locate the start of the trail, walk south from the main parking lot under the power lines, cross Gravenstafel Brook on one of the log jams and head straight up the steep cut-line that parallels the left bank of the stream. After the initial climb, logged-out areas open up. Keep straight ahead here to reach the lake. Avoid a cut-line that branches left up the ridge towards the summit of Mount Haig. At the lake, there is the option of continuing over the saddle of Gravenstafel Ridge and down into Syncline valley. In the spring and early summer there is still snow here, particularly on the Syncline side, so plan accordingly.

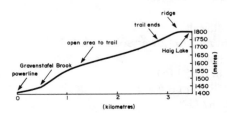

SYNCLINE BROOK

Half-day hike; easy
Length: 5 km (3 mi.) to upper valley
Hiking time: 2½ to 4 hours return
Elevation gain: 150 m (500 ft.)
Maximum elevation: 1600 m (5300 ft.)
Map: Mount Head 82 J/7
Access: Turn right off Highway 774, 3 km before West Castle Ski Area and just short of the small bridge over Syncline Brook. Park here.

Syncline valley, with its rushing brook and fine scenery, is a good choice for a relaxed, half- or full-day hike. In spring, run-off brooks send long trails of spray over the sides of Syncline Mountain, Mount St. Eloi and Gravenstafel Ridge. The rich, moist valley supports many wildflowers, shrubs and dense patches of skunk cabbage. The moderate terrain, together with the option of crossing the saddle of Gravenstafel Ridge to Haig Lake, allow you to choose the best route and timing according to prevailing weather and snow conditions. Some care must be taken at the fords on Syncline Brook (narrow, thigh deep, fast flowing). In June some snow and avalanche debris encroach on sections of the path, but these are easily traversed or skirted.

The four-wheel-drive road is easy to follow as it heads straight up the valley. It holds to the right of Syncline Brook for 1 km, crossing briefly to the other side. Just before the second ford, beneath the scree slopes of Gravenstafel Ridge, is a fine campsite. Immediately past the second ford a particularly impressive waterfall can be seen tumbling off Syncline Mountain. The trail ends in the tall forest at the valley's head, where there is another good camping spot.

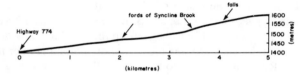

SOUTHFORK LAKES

Day hike/backpack; difficult
Length: 4.5 km (2.8 mi.) to Lower Southfork Lakes
Hiking time: 2 to 5 hours
Elevation gain: 625 m (2050 ft.)
Maximum elevation: 2025 m (6600 ft.)
Map: Beaver Mines 82 G/8
Access: Drive approximately 10 km past the Castle River bridge on West Castle River Road. Follow the gravel access road on the left to the bank of the West Castle River. The trail begins on a cut-line on the east bank of the river, and a very difficult ford is required to reach the trailhead. The trail is visible high on open slopes above West Castle valley. (Take note of this in case trails in the lower valley become hard to follow.)

The dramatic alpine setting of the upper two lakes in their picturesque basin makes this one of the most rewarding hikes in the Castle River area. The hike up to the 2025-m-high basin on Barnaby Ridge is difficult but well worth the effort. The lakes are stocked with rare golden trout, making this a favourite spot with local fishermen. An optional hike follows the entire length of Barnaby Ridge to Grizzly Lake. Numerous peaks (including Southfork Mountain) are easily ascended, offering half-day options from a base at the Southfork Lakes.

The ford of West Castle River is difficult (20 m wide, waist deep, fast flowing), and it is a good idea to search along the bank for the best spot to cross. The trail begins on the east bank, near the foundations of an old wooden bridge, and continues as a cut-line, overgrown with alders, to the base of Barnaby Ridge, where it begins a very steep climb. There are switchbacks at the steepest portion. Eventually the trail opens up on a rock outcropping, where there are views back down to the West Castle River valley, and where the climbing becomes easier. The open slopes are covered with many colourful wildflowers. The trail crosses the ridge and descends through the trees to Lower Southfork Lake. One good campsite is available on the north shore of the lower lake. Or continue up the short, steep ascent to the basin containing Middle and Upper lakes; there are good camping sites on the east sides of both these lakes.

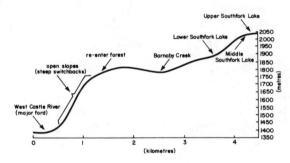

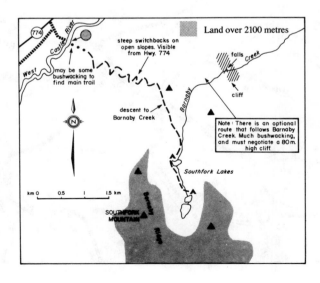

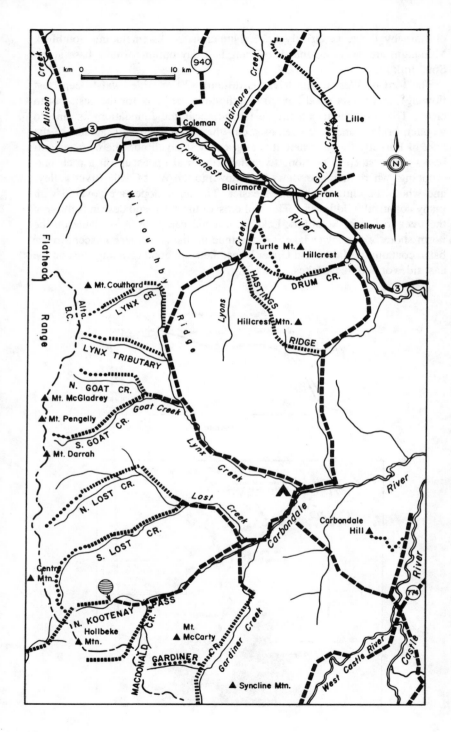

CARBONDALE RIVER AREA

The Carbondale River basin drains that portion of the Rockies west of Pincher Creek. The Carbondale River originates in the alpine meadows below North Kootenay Pass, and its major tributaries include Lynx and Gardiner creeks. The sources of the Carbondale and its tributaries are high cirques in the Flathead and Clark ranges along the Continental Divide. The Carbondale River flows into the Castle River as it leaves the mountains just beyond Carbondale Hill. The broad valleys of the Carbondale and its tributaries were shaped by alpine glaciation.

The name "Carbondale" refers to the area's Mesozoic coal deposits, formed over 65 million years ago. During the late Jurassic and Cretaceous periods, plant and animal life flourished in the tropical climate of that part of North America which now forms the prairies. Gradually seas encroached on the land, and this jungle vegetation was buried beneath newly deposited marine sediment, to form today's coal deposits. The uplifting of the Rocky Mountains at the end of the Cretaceous period exposed the coal, providing the impetus for mining by early white settlers.

Alberta Forest Service campsites include Castle River Bridge, Lynx Creek and Castle Falls. Main access to hiking trails in the area is provided by the Carbondale River Road, which begins in Hillcrest.

Upper Lynx Creek basin and Mount Coulthard

CARBONDALE FIRE LOOKOUT

Half-day hike; easy
Length: 3.5 km (2.2 mi.) to lookout
Hiking time: 1 to 2 hours to lookout
Elevation gain: 460 m (1500 ft.)
Maximum elevation: 1800 m (5900 ft.)
Map: Beaver Mines 82 G/8
Access: Drive approximately 3 km on the Castle River Falls Road from Highway 774. A sign marks the beginning of the trail. Park here; an access gate prohibits vehicular travel.

This steep road to the Carbondale Fire Lookout provides an easy half-day hike—easy in terms of distance, not elevation gain. However, the panoramic view from the lookout is well worth the effort. Numerous recognizable mountains to the south and east include Syncline Mountain, Gravenstafel Ridge, Barnaby Ridge, Whistler Mountain and Table Mountain, and there are excellent views of the Castle River valley.

The route climbs steadily on a restricted access road for the entire distance. Forest cover limits the views, but occasionally vistas open to the south towards Syncline Mountain, Gravenstafel Ridge and Barnaby Ridge. Near the summit, the trees thin out and the lookout tower becomes visible ahead. The summit with its panoramic views is reached after a final short rush up the slope. The existing lookout was built in 1953, but the foundation of the original lookout, built in 1929, remains. The two-storey building has living quarters on the main floor and fire detection equipment on the second. During the summer months an attendant is on duty, and all visitors are invited to sign a guest book.

GARDINER CREEK

Day hike; moderate to difficult
Length: 14 km (8.4 mi.) to upper valley
Hiking time: 5 to 7 hours return
Elevation gain: 725 m (2300 ft.)
Maximum elevation: 2200 m (6950 ft.)
Maps: Beaver Mines 82 G/8; Upper Flathead 82 G/7
Access: Drive the Carbondale River Road to Lynx Creek Campground. Continue up the Carbondale River, crossing four bridges. One kilometre beyond the fourth bridge on the left-hand (south) side of the road is the Gardiner Creek Road. The first 3 km are driveable, ending with a washed-out bridge. Park along the roadside.

This straightforward hike to the headwaters of Gardiner Creek follows a well-defined route through a spruce forest mixed with stands of aspen. The trail ends at the headwalls surrounding the creek's source. Syncline Mountain and Gravenstafel Ridge can be seen from the basin below the headwall. There is no defined trail over the headwall, and only experienced climbers should venture beyond there.

An option for reaching the Alberta–British Columbia border is via a rough dirt road from the lower Gardiner Creek valley. Turn west onto a dirt road at the 8-km point and make a stiff 4-km hike to the Continental Divide ridge. The views from the ridge extend in all directions. There is the added option for a ridge walk around Mount McCarty.

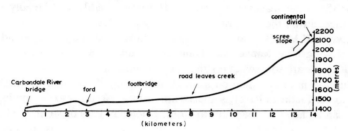

MACDONALD CREEK

Half-day hike; moderate
Length: 4.3 km (2.7 mi.) to pass
Hiking time: 1½ to 2½ hours
Elevation gain: 330 m (1100 ft.)
Maximum elevation: 1900 m (6200 ft.)
Map: Upper Flathead 82 G/7
Access: Drive the Carbondale River Road from Hillcrest for 29 km, 10 km past Lynx Creek Recreational Area. Cross Carbondale River five times after the campground and, from the south bank, head west towards North Kootenay Pass. The trailhead is at an old logging road (not accessible by vehicle) several hundred metres before the MacDonald Creek bridge. Adequate parking is available at the trailhead.

This hike leads along abandoned logging and seismic roads to a steep and rocky pass over the Continental Divide at the head of MacDonald Creek valley. The trail/logging road begins at the Carbondale River Road and heads south through a burned-out area. Some spruce have regenerated in the lower valley, and there is a lot of brush (alders and willows) along the route. Strawberries, raspberries and blueberries are plentiful when in season, so be alert for bears.

A large earth mound across the road prohibits vehicular travel. Locate what appears to be the most major of a maze of logging and seismic roads and follow it to a level, open area. The road starts to swing to the right (south-west) and the pass will be visible. Several small runoff streams are easily crossed. The road then passes through an abandoned sawmill site, and the route is picked up again at the north end. Take the right-hand fork after the sawmill and cross MacDonald Creek (3 m wide, ankle deep), which can usually be forded on rocks or on a log. The road switchbacks steeply to rise above a small ridge, and when it levels out, there is a good view of the pass and of more steep switchbacks ahead. The grade steepens as the road passes through a forest of large Douglas-firs.

Now the route leaves the forest and climbs steadily and steeply over a rocky road. From the crest of the pass are good views of the scenic Carbondale River and MacDonald Creek valleys. Views east and north extend as far as the Livingstone Range and Thunder Mountain. Views westward down Pollock Creek are somewhat restricted by the terrain.

An option is to continue on a rough four-wheel-drive road down Pollock Creek to the Flathead River, some 10 km distant. No trails exist, but highline routes can be taken either north to North Kootenay Pass or south to Gardiner Creek. Although the elevation here is only 1900 m, the pass is susceptible to very strong winds and may be much colder than expected. Warm clothing is recommended.

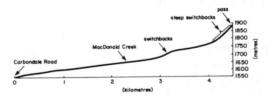

NORTH KOOTENAY PASS

Half-day hike; moderate
Length: 4 km (2.5 mi.) to pass
Hiking time: 1½ to 2½ hours to pass
Elevation gain: 430 m (1400 ft.)
Maximum elevation: 2065 m (6776 ft.)
Map: Upper Flathead 82 G/7
Note: There is no water in the immediate vicinity of the pass, and this route can be tiring on a warm day.
Access: From Hillcrest, follow the Carbondale River Road to its end on the banks of the river. Drive up the road past the MacDonald Creek trailhead (10 km past Lynx Creek Campground). This road may be blocked by winter snows as late as mid-June. The road continues past MacDonald Creek and

begins to climb. Take the right (lower) fork to the road end on a bank above the Carbondale River. The trail begins on the grassy slope (overgrown cut-line) on the opposite (north) side of the river, and can be reached only by a swift and icy ford. If you find that the road ends at an old sawmill site with large slash piles, you have taken the wrong fork.

This scenic trip follows a historically significant route. North Kootenay Pass was used regularly by Kootenay Indians on their migrations across the Rockies. The first white man to record a crossing of the pass was Lt. Thomas Blakiston, a member of the Palliser Expedition, in August of 1858. In addition to its historical appeal, the trail offers excellent views from the alpine environs of the Flathead and Carbondale valleys. A good option exists to continue over a small pass northeast of North Kootenay Pass into the South Lost Creek drainage. Another route continues over North Kootenay Pass to the Flathead River valley. Two cars are required for either option.

From the trailhead, an overgrown cut-line is visible on the opposite side of the Carbondale River. To reach it, ford the icy-cold Carbondale (10 m wide, knee to thigh deep, fast-flowing). Take extra care in crossing: ropes, staffs and running shoes are recommended. Once across the river, follow the open slopes that lead back to the right for approximately 100 m. This direction appears to be wrong, but the cut-line soon swings back to the left (west) and heads towards North Kootenay Pass.

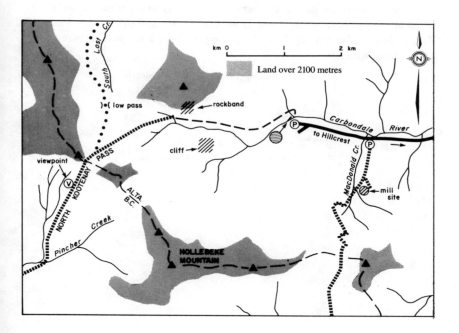

There is no definable trail, but the route is obvious through the tall grass of the cut-line, and hiking is easy. Open logged-out areas are visible across the valley on the opposite side of the Carbondale River. The trail soon becomes more defined, and a faint track joins it from the valley below. Continue straight, following the cut-line as it passes a recent avalanche path. Across the valley a large cliff face is visible. Now the trail passes below a rock band (uphill to the right) and continues straight. The cut-line swings to the left (west), and North Kootenay Pass is visible ahead. As the cut-line emerges above the tree line, it widens to road width and proceeds steadily up towards the pass, flanked by open scree slopes. There are superb views back down the Carbondale River valley. A steep climb leads to the summit, indicated by a cement and tin marker. Continuing on, catching views of the Flathead Valley, one can appreciate the words of magnetic observer Thomas Blakiston, who in 1858 wrote:

> . . . a few steps further and I gave a wild shout as I caught the first glimpse in a deep valley, as it were at my feet, of a feeder of the Pacific Ocean. It was the Flathead River, a tributary of the Columbia. At the same moment the shots of my men's guns echoing among the rocks announced the passage of the first white man over Kootanie Pass.

Blakiston's aneroid barometer showed an altitude of 5960 feet, over 800 feet lower than the actual elevation.

The road enters the pass and emerges on a grassy knoll amid stunted trees, an ideal lunch spot, where there is an excellent panorama of the Flathead Valley. The road continues down from the pass for 4 km, eventually reaching the Flathead River.

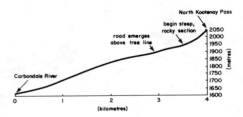

54

SOUTH LOST CREEK

Day hike; moderate
Length: 8.5 km (5.3 mi.) to pass
Hiking time: 4 hours to pass
Elevation gain: 490 m (1600 ft.)
Maximum elevation: 1970 m (6500 ft.)
Maps: Upper Flathead 82 G/7; Beaver Mines 82 G/8
Access: Drive the Carbondale River Road for approximately 4 km past the Lynx Creek Campground (crossing Carbondale River four times after the campground) to Lost Creek Road. Head north on this road for approximately 4 km, to the trailhead at the junction of North and South Lost creeks. Park here.

The South Lost Creek trail heads left (southwest) from the junction and leads through a scenic valley at the base of the imposing and spectacular walls of the Flathead Range. An excellent option is to continue over a 1970-m pass at the end of the South Lost Creek valley into the headwaters of the Carbondale River and the North Kootenay Pass area. Experienced route-finders might choose to cross the low ridge separating North and South Lost creeks, and descend to the North Lost Creek drainage.

Hiking the first 6 km of this route along an old logging road is easy and straightforward. You will cross South Lost Creek twice on bridges in the first 3 km as you draw closer to the sheer cliffs of Centre Mountain. Continue on the north side of the creek; the logging road begins to swing to the southwest, passing though a burned-out forest. Some spruce trees remain, but lodgepole pines have repopulated much of the lower valley. As the road continues its southwesterly course, paralleling the Flathead Range, it passes a number of small but beautiful waterfalls on tributary streams.

At the 6-km mark, the logging road ends. From here to the pass it is a matter of bushwhacking and route-finding. The general direction is obvious (southwest), and the forest is fairly open. Despite this, you should carry a topographic map and compass; rain and low clouds can quickly obscure landmarks.

The forest cover ends within a kilometre of the road's end, and the route steeply ascends to the pass through varied terrain of rockslides, brush and alpine meadows. Wildflowers abound throughout the valley. Glacier lilies dominate in the early season, colouring many of the avalanche slopes a brilliant yellow.

Ascend the valley, picking the line of least resistance; return to the main creek if problems arise. The best option is to choose a highline route that will avoid underbrush. Be sure to stay away from the snow and rock slopes directly beneath the cliffs of the Flathead Range, as loose rocks frequently fall from the main face.

From the alpine meadows at the summit, the views towards North Kootenay Pass and the South Lost Creek valley are excellent. It is little more than a kilometre to North Kootenay Pass over open slopes to the northwest, and approximately 3 km southeast to the North Kootenay Pass trailhead.

For those interested in taking the North Kootenay Pass–South Lost Creek option, it is worthwhile beginning at the North Kootenay Pass trailhead, to take advantage of the large elevation loss while descending the South Lost Creek valley. Two vehicles are required, to save approximately 11 km of hiking on access roads.

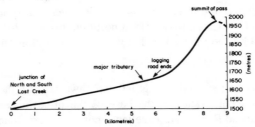

NORTH LOST CREEK

Day hike; difficult
Length: 9.2 km (5.5 mi.) to lakes
Hiking time: 5 to 8 hours for loop
Elevation gain: 480 m (1525 ft.)
Maximum elevation: 2020 m (6400 ft.)
Maps: Beaver Mines 82 G/8; Upper Flathead 82 G/7
Access: Follow the Carbondale River Road from Hillcrest. Four kilometres west of Lynx Creek Campground, turn north onto Lost Creek Road and drive 4 km to the junction of North and South Lost creeks. Park here; the road is in poor condition beyond this point.

This otherwise uneventful hike has a rewarding end at three small lakes in a basin at the headwaters of North Lost Creek. A recommended option is to follow a tributary of North Lost Creek, cross a low ridge and descend to the lakes. Keep in mind that snow often remains in much of the upper valleys until early summer.

The beginning of this hike, at the junction of North and South Lost creeks, is not particularly attractive as much of the lower valley has been extensively logged. Leave the main road as it heads up a tributary of North Lost Creek at the 4.4-km mark. (A fine waterfall is visible on the tributary stream.) From the fork, a rough road follows North Lost Creek until the 7.0-mark. When the road ends, continue southwest along the course of the creek, route-finding as you go, and eventually making a steep climb into a cirque containing a small lake.

From this cirque, you now must cross the low ridge to the north. Find the easiest route to the ridge crest and descend to the forested basin containing the three lakes. Exercise caution when returning to the main North Lost Creek as several steep drops must be negotiated. Once in the valley bottom, it is simply a matter of retracing your steps back to the trailhead.

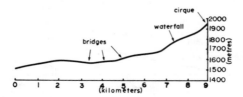

GOAT CREEK (South Fork)

Half-day hike; easy
Length: 3.5 km (2 mi.) to upper valley
Hiking time: 1 to 1½ hours to end of trail
Elevation gain: 275 m (900 ft.)
Maximum elevation: 1850 m (6100 ft.)
Map: Upper Flathead 82 G/7
Access: Drive Lynx Creek Road for approximately 9 km from the Carbondale River Road. (Lynx Creek Road begins on the east side of Lynx Creek.) Turn left onto Goat Creek Road. Continue for 3.5 km; the road has several bad sections (mudholes in early season) and becomes impassable at the north fork of Goat Creek. Park here. The trailhead for the south fork of Goat Creek is at the footbridge over Goat Creek's north fork.

This pleasant hike leads through a quiet forest to open avalanche slopes at the base of Mount Darrah. The good views along the steep cliff-face of the Flathead Range make this hike worthwhile. Options exist for those with route-finding experience to continue north into the drainage of the north fork of Goat Creek, or south into the North Lost Creek drainage.

After crossing the wooden footbridge over the north fork of Goat Creek, take the middle (uphill) fork. As this road begins to swing left towards the south fork of Goat Creek, turn right onto an old logging road heading up the north side of the creek. A pile of debris obscures the beginning of the road. If you miss the old road, backtrack approximately 75 m from the bridge over the south fork of Goat Creek. The creek is a constant companion along the entire distance of the hike but is never crossed.

There are several good views of Mount Darrah and the Flathead Range from the road. The valley has been extensively logged, and you will pass a number of abandoned sawmill sites. The route becomes a single-file trail on an old roadbed strewn with numerous large deadfalls. The trail passes below some logged areas which open up to present views of an ominous rock face, and ends at a small creek just past a clearcut area. Follow an ill-defined trail on the north side of the creek through open brush onto avalanche slopes 200 m to 300 m ahead. From slopes under the towering cliffs of Mount Darrah you will have views in all directions.

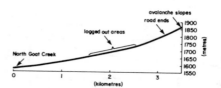

GOAT CREEK (North Fork)

Half-day hike; easy to moderate
Length: 2.5 km (1.5 mi.) to upper valley
Hiking time: 2 to 3 hours return
Elevation gain: 95 m (300 ft.)
Maximum elevation: 1770 m (5600 ft.)
Map: Upper Flathead 82 G/7
Note: Lynx Creek Road is not in prime condition, and low-clearance vehicles are not recommended.
Access: Drive approximately 9 km on Lynx Creek Road from the Carbondale River Road and turn left onto Goat Creek Road. Continue for 3.5 km to the north fork of Goat Creek and park. Goat Creek Road can be impassable when wet.

From the trailhead this short hike leads through a forest of spruce and Douglas-fir. A scramble to a ridge on the Continental Divide is an option for those with the time and energy. From the ridge between Mount Pengelly and Mount McGladrey, impressive views extend west into British Columbia, and south along the Flathead Range.

The trailhead begins at the footbridge over the north fork of Goat Creek. Immediately there is a four-way intersection; take the right fork and proceed past a pile of logs that serves as a vehicular barrier.

Proceed for approximately 1.5 km through logged-out areas, then veer left away from the creek and follow the base of a spur through enclosed forest and thick undergrowth.

The road returns to creek level, crosses the north fork of Goat Creek and ends after a few hundred metres. Those wishing to continue to the ridge must bushwhack through open slopes to a rocky cirque. From the cirque, you can scramble up to the rocky saddle on the Continental Divide.

LYNX TRIBUTARY

Half-day hike; easy
Length: 3.6 km (2 mi.) to end of trail
Hiking time: 1 to 2 hours to avalanche slopes
Elevation gain: 180 m (600 ft.)
Maximum elevation: 1740 m (5700 ft.)
Map: Crowsnest 82 G/10
Note: Lynx Creek Road is not in prime condition, and low-clearance vehicles are not recommended. If the first kilometre after the Carbondale River Road gives you trouble, turn around—it doesn't get better.
Access: Drive 29 km (Mile 18) on the Lynx Creek Road from the Carbondale River Road. (Signs on the trees indicate mileage travelled.) At Mile 18 an old logging road forks left, leading down to Lynx Creek. Park here.

This hike along a small tributary of Lynx Creek comes close to the impressive rock faces of the Flathead Range and gives excellent views of Mount McGladrey. Sections of corduroy road built by logging companies are still visible.

From the trailhead, follow the old logging road down to Lynx Creek. No bridge remains over the creek, but you can get across on one of the numerous logs. Continue along the winding dirt road that leads towards the Flathead Range. Much of the route passes through open areas, some logged-out, some burnt. Forest regeneration is beginning in most of the cleared areas. The good views of Mount McGladrey and Mount Coulthard are fewer as the forest cover becomes denser. Approximately 1.5 km from Lynx Creek is an old bridge made of large logs and rocks. Beyond this point, numerous small runoff streams are encountered, but are easily forded. Half a kilometre farther on, the logging road ends and a trail beings. The trail becomes obscure as it enters a sheltered area with a moist forest floor and much flora. The route is marked with orange flagging tape, and eventually comes to a creek bed on the left. Follow the creek bed to open avalanche slopes that show signs of recent damage. This is the end of the route, but those with an adventuresome spirit can explore the slopes. Be alert as bears often browse for berries or grub for insects here.

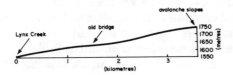

LYNX CREEK

Half-day hike; easy
Length: 5.6 km (3.5 mi.) to upper valley
Hiking time: 1½ to 2½ hours to end of trail
Elevation gain: 120 m (400 ft.)
Elevation loss: 90 m (300 ft.)
Maximum elevation: 1740 m (5700 ft.)
Map: Crowsnest 82 G/10
Note: Lynx Creek Road is not in prime condition, and low-clearance vehicles are not recommended. If the first kilometre after the Carbondale River Road gives you trouble, turn around—it doesn't get better.
Access: Drive the Lynx Creek Road for approximately 31 km from the Carbondale River Road. (Lynx Creek Road begins on the east side of Lynx Creek at its junction with the Carbondale River.) At 31 km, a road forks left (northwest) and downhill. This is the trailhead. Park at the fork; the road up Lynx Creek soon becomes impassable.

The Lynx Creek trail leads to the base of Mount Coulthard and the Flathead Range and the headwaters of Lynx Creek. It is an excellent choice for an afternoon's outing. Except for the final half-kilometre, the route follows logging roads and presents no problems. Much of the logged-out area has regrown and provides excellent browsing for deer. The openness of the forest cover affords excellent views of the Flathead Range, and in particular, Mount Coulthard. Lynx Creek is a constant companion for much of the hike.

At the trailhead there are views west to Mount Coulthard and north to Crowsnest Mountain, guarding Crowsnest Pass. The road quickly descends to the valley bottom. At the first fork, take the road to the right, which climbs a small hill. Once on the valley bottom the road swings left (west) and passes through a logged area where trees are regenerating. Several minor roads fork to the right. Stay on the main road which follows the course of Lynx Creek. Several small tributaries must be crossed, and may be in flood early in the season, but they pose no problems other than causing wet feet. An old mill site is visible through the trees on the opposite side of the creek. Continue on the north side of the creek and pass the remains of an old log cabin and, soon after, a natural spring. At a major fork in the road, take the right fork (the less likely looking one), which is more of a footpath; in a short distance it rejoins the main road, and saves crossing Lynx Creek twice. Soon another mill site is passed and the road eventually ends in fallen timber. From here there is little in the way of well-defined trails, but the route is obvious. Pick your way through fallen trees until you reach a small creek, the headwaters of Lynx Creek, where there are good views of Mount Coulthard and the Flathead Range. Cross the creek on rocks and continue up the creek bed through some underbrush to a seismic cut-line. A distinct trail follows the cut-line left uphill to its end on open slopes at the base of the Flathead Range. In season, these flower-covered slopes provide an excellent spot from which to survey the surrounding area. Looking back down Lynx Creek and across to Willoughby Ridge, the Ironstone Lookout is visible. As with other hikes along the Flathead Range, the proximity of the cliffs to the west means that the sun sets much earlier than in main valleys, and snow lingers longer in spring.

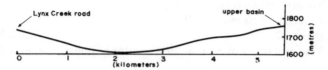

Glacier lilies growing on avalanche slopes along South Lost Creek Trail

HASTINGS RIDGE

Day hike; easy
Length: 11 km (6.8 mi.) one way
Hiking time: 3 to 4 hours one way
Elevation gain: 300 m (1000 ft.)
Elevation loss: 600 m (2000 ft.)
Maximum elevation: 1830 m (6000 ft.)
Map: Blairmore 82 G/9
Note: If hiking as a one-way trip, be sure to arrange transportation at both ends.
Access: Hillcrest access: Drive 6.5 km from Hillcrest on the Carbondale River Road. The trail is a four-wheel-drive road starting on the west side of Carbondale River Road. Lyons Creek Access: drive 4 km south from Blairmore on the Lyons Creek Road. The trail starts on the left-hand side of the road.

This trail follows a rough four-wheel-drive road which has been used recently for seismic testing. It wanders through a mixed forest and climbs gradually in the first kilometre, opening up to view the valley of a Byron Creek tributary. The road winds around the base of Hillcrest Mountain and climbs Hastings Ridge. From here there are views north to Turtle Mountain and the Crowsnest valley.

Along the next section are coal seams and uniquely eroded rock formations. The road heads south for a short distance and then turns east, with views of Ironstone Lookout, Mount Coulthard, Andy Good Peak and Mount McLaren. It continues through rolling meadows for approximately 2 km before descending to its end at the Lyons Creek Road.

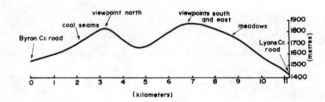

DRUM CREEK (Turtle Mountain Circuit)

Half-day hike; moderate
Length: 6 km to Lyons Creek Road; 8 km to Blairmore
Hiking time: 3 to 5 hours to Blairmore
Elevation gain: 275 m (900 ft.)
Elevation loss: 335 m (1100 ft.)
Maximum elevation: 1650 m (5400 ft.)
Map: Blairmore 82 G/9
Access: (See Hillcrest map.) From Highway 3, take the main road into
Hillcrest. One-and-a-half blocks past the bridge over Drum Creek, turn right
at the trailer park and watch for a large open field on the left side of the
road. At the end of the field turn left onto a dirt road and continue driving
up a steep hill. Keep right at the fork and pass several old mine buildings.
Drive as far as Drum Creek, the trailhead. Park at the side of the road, as
parking space is limited. This hike will require two cars, or a long walk
from Blairmore to Hillcrest to retrieve your car.

Pleasant forests and bubbling creeks will accompany you for most of this
hike. Three kilometres from the trailhead, there is the option of continuing on
a rough road over a low ridge to the Lyons Creek Road (Ridge Route) or
taking a trail over a low pass that emerges on the Lyons Creek Road a few
kilometres closer to Blairmore (North Fork).

The route begins on the south side of Drum Creek. Follow the rough road
(impassable for vehicles) that parallels the creek. Continue past the small
falls and pool, reaching a cement dam and pumphouse. Beyond here the
creek (3 m wide, ankle deep) crosses the road several times. Sometimes logs
and rocks serve as makeshift bridges; at other times the creek must be waded.
From the open hillsides along Drum Creek are good views north to Turtle
Mountain and south to Hillcrest Mountain. The road climbs onto the open
hillside, about 30 m above the creek in the valley bottom, with a canyon
visible ahead. The road levels out, then descends to creek level and passes
through an open area that was extensively burned a number of years ago. A
gate blocks the road: go through, but be sure to close it behind you! The road
passes through a wide canyon and after a short ascent reaches a fine viewpoint of Drum Creek valley. The road drops again to creek level, passing a
series of beaver ponds, then swings right up the north fork of Drum Creek,
continuing on the east bank.

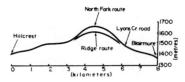

DRUM CREEK (North Fork Option)

Where the road crosses the north fork of Drum Creek, a distinct but unmarked trail continues along the creek's east bank, rising at a moderate grade through dense pine forest. Drum Creek at this point is reduced to a mere trickle, even in spring. The trail often becomes indistinct, so stay close to the valley bottom and continue up the obvious basin. Pass through a small meadow and into a thick spruce forest at the summit of the pass and the drainage divide. The descent from the pass is steep, and the trail is in places ill defined and strewn with deadfall, though there are blazes on trees along the route. The route continues on the north side (right-hand bank descending) of a small creek, until it reaches a large cut-line. It then follows the cut-line's left-hand side, paralleling it for some distance before swinging left (west) into the forest. Keep left at a major fork in the trail. The main trail soon emerges onto a four-wheel-drive road. Follow this road for approximately 200 m and turn right onto Lyons Creek Road. Blairmore is 2 km down the road.

DRUM CREEK (Ridge Route)

After crossing the north fork of Drum Creek, the road begins a steep ascent of the ridge. The road swings south, affording good views back down Drum Creek valley, which is framed by Turtle and Hillcrest mountains. It then switches back north and continues a steady ascent of the ridge through a spruce and pine forest. At the ridge crest a superb panorama greets hikers. The Flathead Range, High Rock Range and Crowsnest Mountain form an impressive backdrop to the forested Willoughby and McGillivray ridges.

Fifty metres from the crest, take the left fork and begin a steep descent, with good views down Lyons Creek valley. An easily forded creek crosses the road several times. The road emerges on the Lyons Creek Road approximately 3.8 km south of Blairmore.

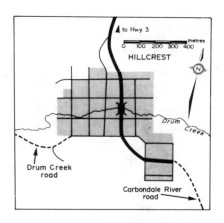

Crowsnest Mountain from Star Creek viewpoint

Bonnie Bentley

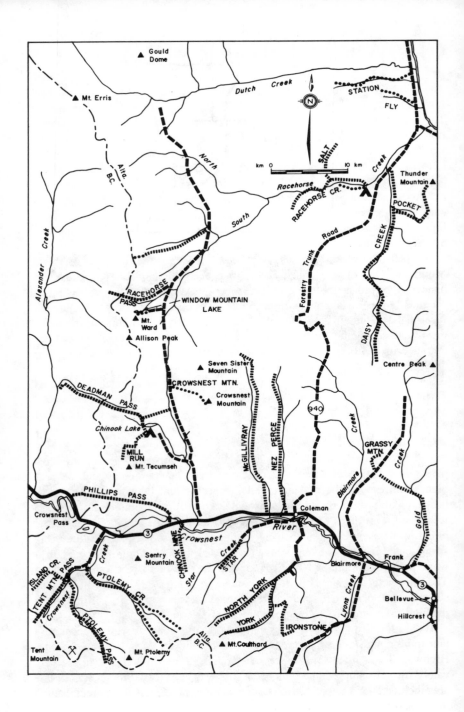

CROWSNEST RIVER AREA

The name "Crowsnest" is translated from the Cree "kah-ka-ioo-wut-tshis-tun" and the Blackfoot "ma-sto-eeas" meaning "where the crows nest." The name was first used by white men in reports of the 1858 Palliser Expedition. It now refers to the pass, river, lake, town and mountain. The Crowsnest River, which flows east out of Crowsnest Lake through the Crowsnest valley, is joined by several tributary creeks from the north and south before its confluence with the Oldman River east of Massacre Butte.

Crowsnest Mountain, its 2785-m summit standing in stark contrast to its surroundings, may be seen in the distance from virtually all directions. Geologically termed a klippe, this prominent peak is an isolated remnant of underlying bedrock displaced from the west.

Another interesting geological feature in the area is the rockslide of Turtle Mountain. One of the largest and most spectacular landslides in Canadian history occurred at the town of Frank on 29 April 1903. In less than 100 seconds, an estimated 99 million tonnes of rock crashed down the eastern face of the mountain, blocking the Crownsest River and burying the road, the Canadian Pacific mainline, the southern end of Frank townsite and the entrance of the Frank coal mine. The rubble covered 3 km and lay 14 m thick. Seventy people were buried in the slide.

The explanation for such a catastrophe lies in the geological structure of Turtle Mountain and the naturally unstable conditions which had developed. The mountain is composed largely of limestone which has inherent planes of weakness in the horizontal bedding planes and the vertical joints. Steeply sloped Turtle Mountain was formed when the limestone strata were tightly folded into an anticline, or arch, during the mountain-building period. With passage of sufficient time, water seeped into the horizontal and vertical planes and eroded the rock internally. Freezing and thawing of this water broke up the solid rock, and seasonal and daily temperature fluctuations weakened it further. These factors created an unstable situation and, combined to a lesser degree with local mining activity, contributed to the catastrophic and inevitable event. Huge slabs of rock failed along the mountain's weak points, and almost "flowed" up the far side of the Crowsnest valley. The enormous distance which the boulders travelled has led geologists to suggest that perhaps trapped and compressed air acted as a frictionless medium over which rocks of such immense size could travel.

Today, the Crowsnest valley is a popular tourist spot, as well as an important mining and logging centre. Several communities lie in the valley along Highway 3 and offer various services and facilities. In addition to the privately owned campgrounds along the highway, provincial campsites in the area include Island Lake, Allison Creek, Chinook Lake and Lundbreck Falls.

GOLD CREEK

There are two possible routes to the historic town of Lille; with adequate transportation they can be combined.

LILLE–GOLD CREEK (Frank Access)

Half-day; moderate
Length: 8 km (5 mi.) to Lille
Hiking time: 1½ to 2½ hours
Elevation gain: 180 m (600 ft.)
Maximum elevation: 1500 m (4900 ft.)
Map: Blairmore 82 G/9
Note: Lille has been designated a historic site by the provincial government, and must be left undisturbed.
Access: Turn north off Highway 3 east of Frank at Gold Creek. Follow the paved road for approximately 1.5 km and park at a four-wheel-drive dirt road that forks left.

In 1901, J. J. Fleutot and C. Remy, employees of Gold Fields Ltd. of British Columbia, were prospecting for gold on Gold Creek but found instead major coal deposits. The company began work on the coal seams that same year and, with French capital, Fleutot organized the West Canadian Collieries Ltd. A railway from Frank was completed in 1903, and production at the mines started immediately; daily output reached 750 tonnes within a few years.

The town grew rapidly. In 1906 it had a hospital, a post office, a four-room schoolhouse and a hotel, and the 1911 census shows a population of 303.

In 1913, the world coke market suffered a drastic decline, and the town's boom days were over. West Canadian Collieries closed the mine, and Lille has been a ghost town ever since.

Not much is left of Lille except foundations and the remains of the coal mine's coke ovens. The only obstacle on the hike is a ford at Gold Creek, a tricky feat in spring.

Follow the four-wheel-drive road into the valley bottom and continue in the general direction of the Gold Creek valley. The route can become confusing as it crosses several cut-lines, pastures and other roads. Keep to the road that follows Gold Creek most closely. You must ford the creek twice, one approximately 3 km from the trailhead and again approximately 1.5 km farther. A minor ford of Morin Creek indicates the beginning of Lille townsite. Although it seems to be only a large meadow, close inspection will reveal building foundations, and, in the trees to the left (west) along Gold Creek, remains of the coke ovens.

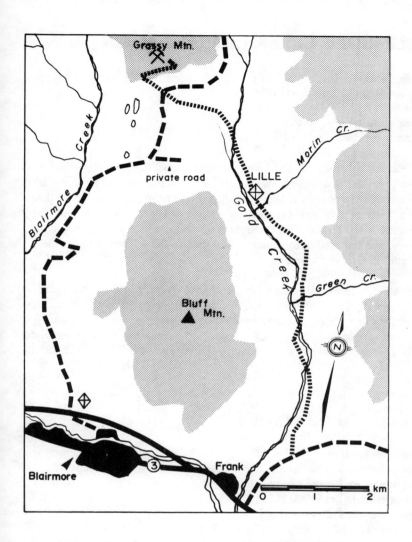

Grassy Mtn.

private road

LILLE

Morin Cr.

Blairmore Creek

Gold Creek

Green Cr.

Bluff Mtn.

N

Blairmore

Frank

3

0   1   2 km

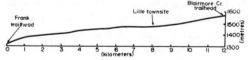

Frank trailhead

Lille townsite

Blairmore Cr. trailhead

1600
1500
1400 (metres)
1300

0 1 2 3 4 5 6 7 8 9 10 11 12
(kilometers)

LILLE–GOLD CREEK (Blairmore Access)

Half-day hike; easy
Length: 3.2 km (1.9 mi.) to Lille
Hiking time: 1 to 1½ hours to Lille
Elevation loss: 60 m (200 ft.)
Maximum elevation: 1540 m (5050 ft.)
Map: Blairmore 82 G/9
Note: Remember that Lille is a historic site and must be left undisturbed.
Access: From the new Blairmore bypass, turn onto the rough road that leads north through the abandoned coal mine, just east of the golf course. Follow it for 6.5 km as it swings around the west side of Bluff Mountain, and park at the crossroad. The road on the right leads to Lille; it is washed out in sections, and impassable to vehicles. The road to the left heads to the old mine site on Grassy Mountain.

The Blairmore to Lille trail is very straightforward, following the route of the old railway line that once ran from the townsite to the mines on Grassy Mountain. Gold Creek is easily crossed on fallen logs. Gold Creek valley opens into a wide meadow at Lille townsite. Among the trees on the right (west) are the coke ovens, and a search of the meadows will uncover building foundations.

IRONSTONE LOOKOUT

Day hike; moderate
Length: 8 km (5 mi.) to top
Hiking time: 2 to 3 hours one way
Elevation gain: 580 m (1900 ft.)
Maximum elevation: 2040 m (6690 ft.)
Map: Crowsnest 82 G/10
Access: (See Coleman map.) Follow York Creek Road for approximately 4 km. The trail starts on the right-hand side of the road, just before the first bridge.

Ironstone is an easy lookout to reach. On a clear day the sweeping view from the top will keep camera bugs snapping for hours.

The trail is a four-wheel-drive road that fords York Creek and begins to follow the York Creek trail. After 3 km the trail forks; continue left on the Ironstone Road, marked by a limited access gate. Climbing steadily for the next 3 km, the trail winds through mixed forest then gradually opens up, giving views of the York Creek and North York Creek valleys to the west.

The final 2 km are constant uphill, with the view ever improving as elevation is gained.

The original 1953 lookout was replaced by the present structure in 1966. Ironstone Lookout is manned from April to October, and visitors are invited to sign a guest book. A topographic map will help to identify the many mountains that can be seen. Crowsnest Mountain is particularly prominent, a silent sentinel to the northwest, guarding the broad valley at its base.

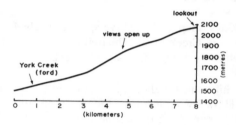

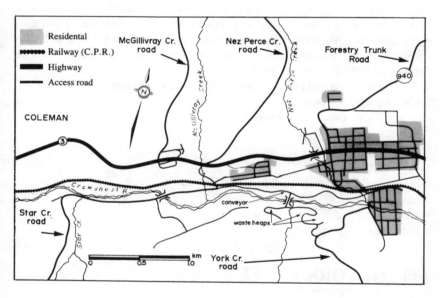

YORK CREEK

Half-day hike; easy
Length: 10 km (6.2 mi.) round trip
Hiking time: 3 to 4 hours return
Elevation gain: 365 m (1200 ft.)
Maximum elevation: 1830 m (6000 ft.)
Map: Crowsnest 82 G/10
Access: (See Coleman map, p.71.) Drive approximately 4 km south from Coleman on the York Creek Road. The trail begins on the right-hand side of the road, just before the bridge across York Creek.

This pleasant hike on a well-defined four-wheel-drive track follows the rolling York Creek valley to the foot of Mount Coulthard.

Approximately 500 m from the trailhead you must ford York Creek (4 m wide, knee deep, medium flowing). Soon you will come to a junction. Turn right onto a more defined road and continue to a second fork where you turn right again and cross York Creek on an old bridge. Follow the road uphill to its end at the remains of a cabin. To the northeast, Ironstone Fire Lookout can be seen atop Willoughby Ridge.

For experienced and energetic hikers there is the option of continuing along York Creek to its source at a small lake on Mount Coulthard. This option requires 2 km of steep bushwhacking.

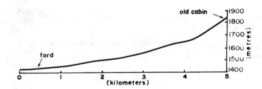

NORTH YORK CREEK

Day hike; easy
Length: 6 km (4 mi.) to basin
Hiking time: 5 to 6 hours
Elevation gain: 305 m (1000 ft.)
Maximum elevation: 1825 m (6000 ft.)
Map: Crowsnest 82 G/10
Access: (See Coleman map, p. 71.) Drive approximately 4 km south from Coleman on the York Creek Road. The trail begins on the right-hand side of the road, just before the bridge across York Creek.

This is a pleasing hike to a basin at the foot of Mount Coulthard. The gradual rise through solid coniferous forest is easily managed, and the views from the basin are splendid. Early-season hikers should be aware that there can be a fair amount of snow on the upper parts of the trail until early June.

Approximately 500 m from the trailhead, ford York Creek (4 m wide, knee deep) and continue west along the trail on the creek's left bank. Where York Creek and North York Creek trails part, follow the lower (North York Creek) trail west up the valley towards an obvious basin. At approximately 3 km there is another ford, and the trail then follows the right bank of North York Creek through a mix of spruce, firs and pines. The trees open in places for quick views of Mount Coulthard. At a bridge crossing on the left, the trail seems to end, but it continues ahead to the right beyond what appears to be a slide, and rejoins the route after about 200 m. Now the trail wanders through the forest until it eventually comes out onto avalanche slopes where there are views east down the valley and up the valley to the basin below Mount Coulthard, Mount Parish, Andy Good Peak and Mount McLaren. The trail ends in the middle of the basin.

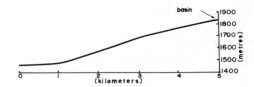

STAR CREEK FALLS

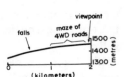

Half-day hike; easy
Length: 2 km (1.2 mi.) to second viewpoint
Hiking time: 1 to 1½ hours
Elevation gain: 95 m (300 ft.)
Maximum elevation: 1485 m (4700 ft.)
Map: Crowsnest 82 G/10
Access: (See Coleman map, p. 71.) Drive approximately 2 km down the Star Creek Falls Road. The trailhead begins on a four-wheel-drive dirt road.

This short and pleasant hike to picturesque falls and canyons offers a satisfying view of the Crowsnest valley and surroundings.

Follow the dirt road left to Star Creek and a foot trail. The well-shaded and moist trail leads 500 m to the base of a 25-m cliff band where Star Creek falls tumble over the cliff from a deep gorge above.

Scramble up the cliff on a faint but safe trail to a viewpoint. Crowsnest

Mountain rises in the south and Star Creek canyon is to the immediate north. From this viewpoint, follow a flagged trail to a second viewpoint from which you can see the headwaters of Star Creek in the Flathead Range to the south.

From the second viewpoint, you can continue up Star Creek via a seismic road, or descend into the canyon and hike downstream to the falls. There are excellent views from the top of the falls.

NEZ PERCÉ CREEK TO MCGILLIVRAY RIDGE

Day hike; moderate
Length: 13 km (8 mi.) round trip
Hiking time: 4 to 5 hours return
Elevation gain: 520 m (1700 ft.)
Maximum elevation: 2165 m (7100 ft.)
Map: Crowsnest 82 G/10
Access: The road to the trailhead starts from Highway 3 between Coleman Collieries and Coleman trailer park. (See Coleman map, p. 71.) Start at McGillivray Creek and follow the rough road for approximately 2.8 km and park at the Forestry Reserve fence.

This hike up a forest-enclosed fire road is rather straightforward, but the views from the top of McGillivray Ridge make it very worthwhile. From the summit you can explore the whole ridge system.

The trail is level for the first kilometre, but after the two fords of Nez Percé Creek, it climbs gently. Keep left at a fork in the road. At the next fork keep right. The trail begins a steadier climb and gradually opens onto meadows. Climb to the top of a steep hill and enjoy the view of McGillivray Ridge on the left. From there, it is a quick jaunt to the base of the ridge. Scramble to the top for excellent views of Wedge Mountain and the Nez Percé Creek valley.

Nez Percé is a name the French applied to all Indians who pierced their noses to insert shell ornaments. In the nineteenth century, the Nez Percés made brief forays into southwestern Alberta from bases in northern Idaho, either for trade or warfare, but made no lasting claims in the area.

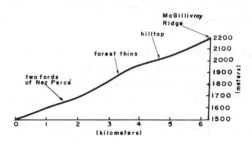

MCGILLIVRAY CREEK

Day hike; moderate
Length: 20 km (12.4 mi.) round trip
Hiking time: 5 to 6 hours return
Elevation gain: 490 m (1600 ft.)
Maximum elevation: 1980 m (6500 ft.)
Map: Crowsnest 82 G/10
Access: (See Coleman map, p. 71.) The trail begins at the Crowsnest Forest
Reserve boundary approximately 2.5 km from the highway along
McGillivray Creek Road.

This pleasant hike leads through the McGillivray Creek valley to the
creek's headwaters at the foot of Seven Sisters Mountain.

From the trailhead, facing north, Wedge Mountain is on your left and
Crowsnest Mountain is straight ahead. Half a kilometre from the trailhead,
take the right fork and continue through stands of lodgepole pines, white
spruce and trembling aspens in the heart of the valley. At the 5-km and 6-km
marks, continue north, passing roads joining from the left. Near the 7-km
point the trail swings east and gradually climbs through a wet, marshy area
towards its end at the base of Seven Sisters Mountain. From the trail end
there is a good view of Ma Butte to the east. Although this is a relatively
simple hike, over a dozen small creeks must be crossed. Never more than
knee-deep, the crossings slow hiking time considerably. Running shoes for
fording, or lots of extra socks are advisable.

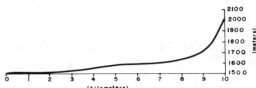

75

ABANDONED MINE TRAIL (Chinook Peak)

Half-day hike; easy
Length: 6 km (3.7 mi.) round trip
Hiking time: 2 to 3 hours return
Elevation gain: 215 m (700 ft.)
Maximum elevation: 1580 m (5200 ft.)
Map: Crowsnest 82 G/10

Access: Park at the Travel Alberta Tourist Information Centre approximately 6 km west of Coleman on the Crowsnest Highway (Highway 3).

The trail begins behind the Information Centre parking lot and follows an old road that once served a coal mine. It crosses an ankle-deep unnamed creek eight times before coming to an intersection of trails. Continue straight, following the trail alongside the creek through a forest of trembling aspen. You will pass the remains of an old car just before the trail opens onto a meadow. Approximately 1 km ahead, where the route forks, is a slag heap, and to the left, over the slag heap, are an abandoned coal mine and several log cabins.

Take the right fork and continue on a single-file path for 2 km to the tree line on Chinook Peak. From there, Crowsnest lake and mountain are visible to the north, and there is a fine view of the lower valley.

PHILLIPPS PASS

Day hike; easy
Length: 4 km (2.5 mi.) to pass; 7 km (4.3 mi.) total to Crowsnest Provincial Park (B.C.) picnic site
Hiking time: 2 to 3 hours to pass
Elevation gain: 180 m (600 ft.)
Maximum elevation: 1550 m (5100 ft.)
Map: Crowsnest 82 G/10
Access: Drive Highway 3 approximately 7 km west of Coleman and turn right onto a road at the east end of Crowsnest Lake. Park on the other side of the Crowsnest River bridge. The trailhead is at the CPR railway crossing. For an alternative access from Crowsnest Provincial Park, drive 2.4 km west of the Alberta–British Columbia border on Highway 3 to the park entrance on the north side of the highway.

The 1550-m Continental Divide pass at the end of this pleasant forest walk is named after Michael Phillipps, a trader for the Hudson's Bay Company, who made the first recorded crossing of the pass in 1873. Phillipps and

Crowsnest passes were used regularly by the Kootenay Indians. Michael Phillipps was a trader on the Kootenay River at Tobacco Plains who began searching for gold in the 1870s. He headed up the Elk River and followed a minor tributary up to the Divide, passing Michel Creek through the gap between Crowsnest Ridge and Phillipps Peak. He is credited with being the first white man to explore the immediate Crowsnest vicinity. In 1879, he was in charge of the crew constructing the first trail through the pass over the same route that the present road follows.

The route begins at the railway crossing, and follows a gravel road through a gate (close it behind you) half a kilometre to a viewpoint overlooking Crowsnest Lake. Here you can expect the wind to sweep up the open hillside along the lake. From the viewpoint, the road climbs steadily to the pass and enters a narrow canyon. There is extensive pine beetle infestation above this canyon. Power lines pass overhead, and the road soon levels out. At the next intersection, take the right fork; the left leads to an AGT station and a transmitter on Crowsnest Ridge. You then pass a gas pipeline monitoring station, and Phillipps Lake, an excellent example of a sink lake, is just ahead. On the road above the lake, a cement block marks the Alberta–British Columbia boundary.

There is the option of returning the way you came or continuing on to British Columbia if transportation has been arranged. Follow the road above the lake as it descends through an enclosed forest of lodgepole pine. Just after the road passes under the power lines, a creek flows out from underground on the right-hand side. A pipeline cut-line opens up the views into British Columbia, and the road widens here. Follow the cut-line to Crowsnest Provincial Park picnic site, which is accessible from Highway 3.

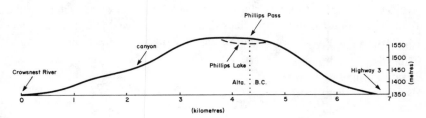

PTOLEMY CREEK

Half-day hike; easy
Length: 4.5 km (2.8 mi.) to upper valley
Hiking time: 1 to 2 hours
Elevation gain: 215 m (700 ft.)
Maximum elevation: 1645 m (5400 ft.)
Map: Crowsnest 82 G/10
Access: Take Highway 3, 1.3 km west of Crowsnest Lake or 0.5 km east of
Island Lake. Turn south onto the Crowsnest Collieries Road and follow it
for 2.5 km until the first turnoff to the left, where a bridge crosses
Crowsnest Creek. The rest of the road is accessible only to four-wheel-drive
vehicles; all others should park at the side of the road just across the
bridge. *POWERLINE DISAPPEARS   PARK AT
CP MILL.   MEADOW*

Although it comes into view only after the first kilometre, the cool waters
of Ptolemy Creek will accompany you on this trail all the way to the valleys
beneath Mount Ptolemy and Andy Good Peak. Beginning at the bridge, the
rocky road rises slowly beside the creek through a mixed forest of spruce,
pine, juniper and aspen. Eventually it opens up to views of Mount Ptolemy
and the Flathead Range, including such recognizable peaks as Andy Good,
Chinook and Mount Coulthard.

Keep to the right where another road joins the route 100 m from the
trailhead. Part of the trail will take you off the rocky road onto a moist, mossy
footpath, the most difficult part coming after about 2.5 km, where a detour
leads across a steep rockslide and the footing is often precarious. You can
avoid this hazard by fording the widest part of the creek and following the
road. The trail leads to two cut-lines that can be followed to upper valleys at
the base of Andy Good Peak and Mount Ptolemy where the route ends amid
open slopes.

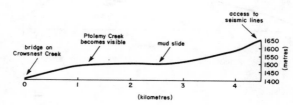

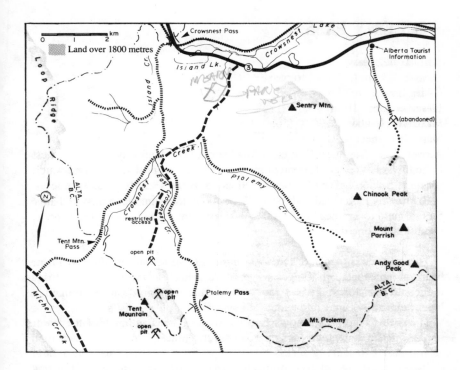

The Flathead Range above Star Creek valley

PTOLEMY PASS

Half-day hike; easy
Length: 4.3 km (2.7 mi.) to pass
Hiking time: 1 to 2 hours
Elevation gain: 210 m (700 ft.)
Maximum elevation: 1700 m (5600 ft.)
Map: Crowsnest 82 G/10
Access: Take Crowsnest Collieries Road south from Highway 3 at Crowsnest Lake towards the Tent Mountain mine site. Obey all posted signs and watch for mine trucks. Drive the gravel road as far as the security gate. Turn left onto Ptolemy Pass Road and follow it for 300 m to a sign that reads: "Change Sides, Yield to Traffic." Park 100 m past the sign, as the road is in very poor condition beyond this point.

The trail leads to a forested 1700-m-high Continental Divide pass in the heart of the Flathead Range. Much of the hike is through an enclosed lodgepole pine forest. Hikers should remember that snow patches remain at higher elevations until mid-June.

The road to the pass follows East Crowsnest Creek in much of the lower section, and the creek crosses the road several times. Stay on the main road as you pass two logging access roads. Keep left at the first fork and right at the second. At a third fork turn left; the road on the right leads in a few hundred metres to a murky reservoir. As the road cuts across semi-open side slopes after a short, steep pitch, the Tent Mountain collieries stand out across the valley, and the reservoir is visible in the basin below the road. Take the right fork at the top of another steep hill, after which the road begins to level out and maintains a moderate grade the rest of the way to Ptolemy Pass. A viewpoint just to the right of the road indicates the pass summit. Mount Pengelly and Mount McGladrey are the prominent peaks in the Flathead Range to the southeast. The rough four-wheel-drive road continues down to Andy Good Creek in British Columbia.

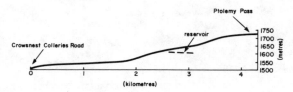

TENT MOUNTAIN PASS

Half-day hike; easy
Length: 4 km (2.5 mi.) to pass
Hiking time: 1½ to 2 hours
Elevation gain: 75 m (250 ft.)
Maximum elevation: 1540 m (5050 ft.)
Map: Crowsnest 82 G/10
Access: Drive the Crowsnest Collieries Road south from Highway 3 at
Crowsnest Lake towards the Tent Mountain mine site. Obey all posted signs
and watch for mine trucks. Park at the security gate.

Tent Mountain Pass is one of the "hidden" Continental Divide passes
flanking the main Crowsnest gap. The low, forested pass is not very picturesque, as it passes close to the mine, but it does provide stark contrast
between wooded Trail Hill to the west and the black coal heaps of the open
pit mine to the east.

Hike the rough four-wheel-drive road that leads to the right from the
security gate; 200 m from the trailhead take the left (south) fork. The trail is
very straightforward after it leaves the mine road. Ankle-deep Crowsnest
Creek crosses the road several times, and the trail skirts several swampy
areas. As the route gently rises towards the pass, you will come close to a
couple of small lakes containing cutthroat trout. Anglers may have trouble
reaching the shoreline through the heavy underbrush. From the pass, views
extending into British Columbia include Michel Creek valley and Mount
Taylor. An option is to continue down Michel Creek on a rough four-wheel-
drive road into British Columbia.

ISLAND CREEK

Half-day hike; easy
Length: 5.5 km (3.4 mi.) one way
Hiking time: 3 to 4 hours return
Elevation gain: 200 m (650 ft.)
Maximum elevation: 1550 m (5400 ft.)
Map: Crowsnest 82 G/10
Access: Drive Highway 3, 10 km west of Coleman and turn south onto
Crowsnest Collieries Road. Obey all posted signs and watch for coal trucks.
Drive 4 km to the mine access gate where the road forks in three. Park here,
as the road is in poor condition beyond this point, and take the right fork,
down Tent Mountain Pass Road.

Following along a well-defined logging road, this hike ends at the 1550-m elevation mark and offers good views of the mountain ranges in the east.

Two hundred metres down the Tent Mountain Pass Road, take the right-hand (north) fork. At the 2.5-km mark, the route joins a logging road coming from the north, and then begins to swing south. Much of the surrounding lodgepole pine and Douglas-fir forest has been logged, but white spruce and trembling aspen saplings are regenerating the area. Wild strawberries and raspberry bushes are also plentiful.

The route forks to the right after 3.5 km and begins a moderate rise. Keep right at the next fork and left at all succeeding forks. If problems arise, always take the fork leading to higher ground. After a final uphill towards Loop Ridge, the road ends at an abandoned logging camp.

The clearings of the former mill sites have exposed much of the hillsides, and the good views extend from the Flathead Range in the southeast to the High Rock Range in the northeast. The parade of peaks southward from Crowsnest Lake are easily identified on a topographic map as Sentry Mountain, Chinook Peak, Mount Parish and Andy Good Peak. The high peak to the south, on the Alberta–British Columbia border, is Mount Ptolemy.

Densely forested Loop Ridge, extending north and south 3 km to 4 km beyond the trail end, offers the option of further exploration along the Alberta–British Columbia border. You can also explore along the skidder trails that lead from each of the clearings.

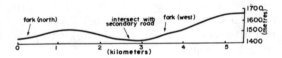

DAISY CREEK

Day hike/backpack; easy
Length: 16.2 km (10 mi.) to upper valley
Hiking time: 5 to 8 hours return
Elevation gain: 400 m (1350 ft.)
Maximum elevation: 1650 m (5350 ft.)
Map: Maycroft 82 G/16
Access: The trailhead is a rough four-wheel-drive road 100 m east of the Daisy Creek bridge on the Forestry Trunk Road, 5.5 km south of Livingstone Ranger Station, or 1 km north of Racehorse Creek Campground.

Novice hikers will appreciate this open valley bottom, and pleasant Daisy Creek is seldom more than a stone's throw away from the trail. Depending on your time and energy, you can easily vary the length of this hike.

Beginning at the rough four-wheel-drive road 100 m east of the Daisy Creek bridge, and heading south, you will soon emerge on a high bench above Daisy Creek. The thick forest cover does limit the views, but you can catch the occasional glimpse of the bubbling creek. The road from here, impassable to vehicles, continues south along the east side of the creek. After one particularly long, straight stretch, you will cross a small tributary (Pocket Creek) entering from the east, and soon after, a road leading left indicates the beginning of the Pocket Creek option. Continue down the main road and ford Daisy Creek (8 m wide, calf deep). There is another ford almost 1 km farther. (Both fords can be avoided by following a rough trail on the left—east—bank of the creek, through brush, encountering a section of loose rock.) After the second ford, the road continues at creek level, passing through some scenic open meadows fringed with poplars. At the 6-km mark you will reach a small but impressive set of falls on Daisy Creek. From here, the trail continues along the creek in the wide valley bottom, through a series of large meadows interspersed with lodgepole pine forest. The view to the east is dominated by the Livingstone Range, which is usually snow-covered until early June.

There is no specific conclusion to this hike. You are free to choose the distance, and this will usually be determined by your energy and the amount of remaining daylight. Remember that the return time will be roughly equivalent to the time in, as there is little elevation loss on the way back. If you choose to remain overnight, numerous suitable campsites are located in the upper valley. Several side trips can be undertaken from the upper valley. For these you will need a topographic map.

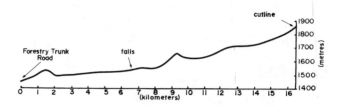

POCKET CREEK

Day hike; easy
Length: 7 km (4.3 mi.); 4 km (2.4 mi.) from Daisy Creek Road
Hiking time: 2 to 3 hours from Forestry Trunk Road
Elevation gain: 450 m (1475 ft.)
Maximum elevation: 1890 m (6200 ft.)
Map: Maycroft 82 G/16
Access: (See Daisy Creek trail, p.82). Pocket Creek trail branches left (east) from Daisy Creek trail, 3 km from the Forestry Trunk Road.

A secluded, forested valley on the east side of Daisy Creek valley is your destination. The open slopes at the end of Pocket Creek trail offer good views of the Livingstone Range, and in particular Thunder Mountain.

The beginning of the hike is a long straight section of Daisy Creek trail. Continue straight after crossing small but fast-running Pocket Creek, and take the left (east) fork immediately prior to the road that descends to Daisy Creek. Pocket Creek trail continues steadily uphill and crosses first a dry creek bed, and then a small stream bridged with stones. The road begins to swing left (north), crosses Pocket Creek, climbs on open slopes dotted with poplar trees and comes to an end on a steep sidehill. Remnants of the road continue for 100 m. The road then switches back to the right, where views open up down Pocket Creek valley and towards the Livingstone Range. Continue up the switchbacking road; Crowsnest Mountain soon can be seen on the western horizon. You might wish to continue up the low hill for the exercise, but views are limited at the top by the forest.

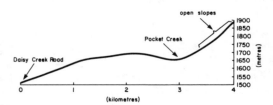

SALT CREEK

Half-day hike; easy
Length: 9.5 km (6 mi.) round trip
Hiking time: 3½ to 4½ hours return
Elevation gain: 610 m (2000 ft.)
Maximum elevation: 1525 m (5000 ft.)
Map: Maycroft 82 G/16

Access: Park at Racehorse Creek Campground, located 25 km north of Coleman on the Forestry Trunk Road, Highway 40. The trailhead is opposite the campground, at the junction of Racehorse and Vicary creeks.

Leading eventually to a fine view of the Racehorse Creek valley, this trail begins as a well-defined cart track on the west bank of Racehorse Creek. Ford the creek (10 m wide, knee to thigh deep) and follow the track west along the opposite bank. You will ford the creek two more times. After the third crossing, take the first right (north) onto a well-maintained road, used regularly to service a well site at the top of the hill to the north. The trail winds up this road through a forest of trembling aspen and white spruce until it reaches the well site. The summit, at an elevation of over 1500 m, affords an excellent view of the Racehorse Creek valley.

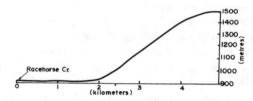

RACEHORSE CREEK CAMPGROUND

Half-day hike; easy
Length: 1.5 km (1 mi.) to end of trail
Hiking time: 1 hour return
Elevation gain: 15 m (50 ft.)
Maximum elevation: 1455 m (4775 ft.)
Map: Maycroft 82 G/16
Access: Park at Racehorse Creek Campground on the Forestry Trunk Road. The trailhead is at the wooden footbridge over Vicary Creek.

Meandering alongside the rushing waters of Racehorse Creek, this trail is perfectly suited for a pleasant evening stroll. The numerous cataracts and rapids and the swiftness of the creek prompted early visitors to call its flow "as quick as a racehorse."

Cross the wooden footbridge and follow the trail through a thick lodgepole pine forest to the south bank of Racehorse Creek. The route is obvious, although it branches into many game trails. If any confusion arises, stay on the trail that remains closest to Racehorse Creek.

Continue along the bank for 1 km to an abandoned beaver dam on a tributary stream. The stream is easily crossed, but the trail becomes less well defined. You would be well advised to turn around here if you are not used to trekking on game trails. For the more adventuresome, the route continues along the south bank through patches of willows on gravel flats before re-entering the forest. The trail fades completely after the next half-kilometre, and if you wish to proceed farther, prepare for heavy bushwhacking.

RACEHORSE CREEK

Half-day hike; easy to moderate
Length: 7.5 km (4.7 mi.) to switchbacks
Hiking time: 3 to 4 hours to valley view
Elevation gain: 60 m (200 ft.)
Maximum elevation: 1500 m (5000 ft.)
Maps: Maycroft 82 G/16; Tornado Mountain 82 G/15
Access: The trail begins at the Racehorse Creek Campground, located approximately 25 km north of Coleman on the Forestry Trunk Road. The trailhead is at the cattle guard where Racehorse Creek must be forded.

Apart from four creek crossings, this is an easy hike, with little elevation gain or loss. The trail begins as a rough four-wheel-drive road which eventually becomes well graded. (After the fourth creek crossing, the route loops back to the Forestry Trunk Road about 9 km south of the campground.) The hiker travels along a wide valley through forests and meadows; hills rise on either side and mountain peaks loom ahead.

The first creek crossing occurs at the trailhead. Once you reach the gravel tracks on the opposite side of Racehorse Creek, the trail is well-defined along its entire length. Ignore all side roads; most simply bring you back to the main road after a detour.

Among the several options, you may choose a short hike to the picnic area in a meadow just past the fourth creek crossing, or, for a longer hike, you may want to follow the narrower portion of Racehorse Creek valley which turns off the main road shortly before the switchback.

FLY CREEK

Half-day hike; moderate
Length: 4 km (2.5 mi.) to second viewpoint
Hiking time: 2 to 3 hours
Elevation gain: 460 m (1500 ft.)
Maximum elevation: 1850 m (6100 ft.)
Map: Maycroft 82 G/16

Access: Drive the Forestry Trunk Road (Kananaskis Road) north from Coleman to the Livingstone Ranger Station. Park at the ranger station and walk back about 0.7 km to the trailhead, about 50 m north of Fly Creek. There is no distinct trail for the first 50 m in from the road.

Fly Creek, accessible along the route, is popular with local fishermen. The trail passes through grassy meadows and a mixed forest of spruce and poplar trees, and climbs to a peak adjacent to Fly Hill, with widespread views of the region. The trail parallels the creek for the first 1.5 km over easy terrain. It then turns away from the creek and begins the steep ascent to the two summits. From the lower summit, the Flathead Range can be seen in the south, and the Livingstone Range is closer in the east. From the upper summit, a view of Fly Hill—the source of Fly Creek—is added to the panorama.

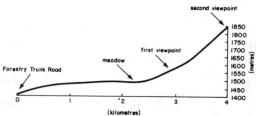

STATION CREEK

Half-day hike; easy to moderate
Length: 3.4 km (2.1 mi.)
Hiking time: 1 to 2 hours
Elevation gain: 215 m (700 ft.)
Maximum elevation: 1615 m (5300 ft.)
Map: Maycroft 82 G/16
Access: Drive the Forestry Trunk Road (Kananaskis Road) north from Coleman to the Livingstone Ranger Station. The trail starts about 100 m north of the ranger station on the west side of the road, where a four-wheel-drive road meets the Kananaskis Road.

The pleasant hike leads through quiet forests and meadows, and several crossings of Station Creek add some challenge and excitement. None of the crossings are difficult as the creek is narrow, shallow and slow flowing, and it might be easier to remove your footwear and wade across.

From the trailhead, the road leads into a mixed forest of pine, aspen and juniper. You can hear the cheerful bubbling of Station Creek long before you reach the water. The road then crosses the creek six times. It is usually possible to cross on stepping stones or fallen logs. (Always be sure the rocks or logs are secure before putting your full weight on them.)

After the last crossing the road ends at a large, open meadow surrounded by trees and hillsides. A game trail that continues through the meadow and into the trees can be followed by those with an adventuresome spirit.

The Livingstone Range is visible on the return trip wherever there are no trees to obstruct the view.

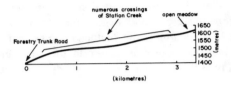

MILL RUN

Half-day hike; easy
Length: 1.6 km (1 mi.) to mill site
Hiking time: ½ to 1 hour
Elevation gain: 120 m (400 ft.)
Maximum elevation: 1600 m (5200 ft.)
Map: Crowsnest 82 G/10
Access: Drive approximately 4 km west of Coleman to the Allison Creek Road and follow the signs to Chinook Lake Campground. The trailhead is at the entrance of the first campsite loop to the left. The trail leaves the campground by the outhouses halfway around the loop.

The Mill Run trail leads to an old mill site marked by a cleared area and the remains of some old buildings. It is one of a network of trails used primarily by cross-country skiers which leads through a forest dominated by fires and lodgepole pines, and offers some views of surrounding mountain peaks, such as Mount Tecumseh and Crowsnest Mountain. This is one of the few hikes in the network that has posted directions; a signpost at each intersection indicates the length of each trail.

The Mill Run is an old gravel road leading approximately 1.6 km to the mill site. Other trails branch off along the route. The first (Junction 5), about 0.8 km from the trailhead, is Marten Trail. Grassy and less travelled, it leads to other junctions, the first only 0.5 km down the trail.

Along the Mill Run, between Junctions 5 and 6, a sign points out a view of Mount Tecumseh. The distance between these two junctions is about 0.6 km. The mill site is 0.2 km beyond Junction 6.

If you are feeling adventurous, continue along the overgrown trail straight through the open area to the site of an old cabin. Broken dishes and tin cans are scattered around and a tin can pile (like no other rubbish pile) forms a wall up the side of a hill.

DEADMAN PASS

Half-day hike; easy to moderate
Length: 7 km (4.2 mi.) to pass
Hiking time: 3½ to 4½ hours return
Elevation gain: 185 m (605 ft.)
Maximum elevation: 1585 m (5200 ft.)
Map: Crowsnest 82 G/10
Access: Drive 4 km west from Coleman on Highway 3. Turn north and continue past the Provincial Fish Hatchery to Chinook Lake Campground. The trailhead is marked by a cross-country ski sign close to the boat ramp.

Despite the ominous name, this is a pleasant trail, consisting of a gentle climb up a series of short rises to the top of the Continental Divide pass.

The trail leaves the campground and passes along the shore of Chinook Lake into the forest. It soon opens into a small clearing by a stream that feeds the lake. Cross the stream on one of several well-made log bridges and follow a rough, marshy road 1.5 km up a damp gully to an intersection with a four-wheel-drive road. Just to the side of the road, you can see a scenic lake with the remains of a logging camp near it. Parts of buildings, stoves, dishes and an old wagon show through the grass. Beside the road, built into the bank, is an old root cellar.

Now continue the four-wheel-drive road up to the pass; ignore the numerous seismic cut-lines that branch off it. Throughout the dense bush you can find the remains of trappers' cabins and lumber camps. Near the top of the pass, the actual watershed and provincial boundary line become blurred by a system of beaver ponds and streams.

The steep scree slope that hems in the trail obscures many of the spectacular views along this route, but you can catch glimpses of Mount Tecumseh, Phillipps Peak and Crowsnest Mountain, and once through the pass you are rewarded with a splendid vista that includes Mount Erickson and stretches of Erickson Ridge.

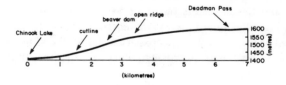

DEADMAN PASS (Allison Creek Road Access)

Access: Drive west from Coleman on Highway 3 for approximately 3 km. Turn right onto Allison Creek Road and follow it for approximately 7 km. The trailhead is on the west side of the road, indicated by a snowmobile route sign.

This route offers alternative access to the Deadman Pass trail. Walk down the road for approximately 1 km to Allison Creek. Cross the creek on the bridge upstream to the right. The trail continues west, intersecting a cut-line at about 1.5 km. (This cut-line can be used as an option to shorten the trip on the way out, but it requires a ford of Allison Creek.) At approximately 2 km this trail begins to parallel a trail coming in from Chinook Lake; gradually they merge into one trail and continue on to Deadman Pass.

CROWSNEST MOUNTAIN

Day hike; difficult
Length: 4 km (2.5 mi.) to summit
Hiking time: 3 to 5 hours return
Elevation gain: 1040 m (3400 ft.)
Maximum elevation: 2785 m (9138 ft.)
Map: Crowsnest 82 G/10
Access: Drive 4 km west from Coleman on Highway 3 and turn north onto the Allison Creek Road for 10.5 km along the west side of Crowsnest and Seven Sisters mountains. The trailhead is marked by a sign on the east side of the road. Parking is available several hundred metres farther up the road.

The variety of terrain between the trailhead and the summit of Crowsnest Mountain makes this a challenging and rewarding hike, and an unparalleled panorama awaits those who manage to reach the summit. The top is a heart-pounding 1040 m above the trailhead, and obstacles along the way include snowfields, rock chimneys and long sections of scree slopes. Therefore, although no actual mountain or rock climbing is required, only proficient rock scramblers should attempt this route. As well, snow patches may remain on the trail until late May, and runoff creeks flow through most coulees (or valleys) until late spring or early summer.

Crowsnest and Seven Sisters mountains are what remain of a displaced sheet of Mississippian limestone moved eastward along the Lewis Thrust. This overthrust sheet is everywhere eroded except for the klippe which forms the chimneys of these two mountains. Some of the limestones are fossil-bearing.

An Alberta Forest Service sign near the trailhead indicates an overall distance of 6 km and a hiking time of 3½ hours. The trail is well-defined, and in the winter doubles as a snowmobile path. Follow the trail through lodgepole pines up the western slope of Crowsnest Mountain. You will cross two seismic cut-lines before the trail narrows and steepens. Continue east, occasionally crossing small creeks. In spring, bright yellow glacier lilies bloom all along it. The trail swings south and east before leaving the forest at the bottom of the open scree slope beneath the north face of Crowsnest Mountain. To the north and east is the western face of Seven Sisters Mountain. Find the trail that leads up the scree slope. Although not obvious, it is discernible and is the best route. No actual climbing will be required, but good scrambling ability is necessary. A short, steep chimney is located at the base of the cliff face. Remember that falling rock is an ever-present danger here. Above the chimney the grade is steep, but the route is obvious all the way to the top. You will have to scramble up some steeper pitches to reach the summit.

The views from the top are outstanding in all directions. The Crowsnest environs (Blairmore, Coleman and Crowsnest Lake) are spread out below. The High Rock Range stands out to the west, and views extend well into British Columbia. To the north, the Livingstone Range is visible, as are the Porcupine Hills to the east and northeast.

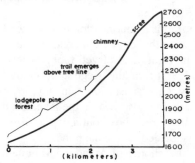

91

WINDOW MOUNTAIN LAKE

Half-day hike; easy
Length: 2 km (1.2 mi.) to lake
Hiking time: 40 minutes to 1 hour
Elevation gain: 210 m (700 ft.)
Maximum elevation: 1980 m (6500 ft.)
Map: Tornado Mountain 82 G/15

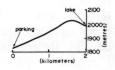

Access: Drive approximately 4 km west of Coleman on Highway 3 and turn right onto Allison Creek Road. Continue right at the junction with Chinook Lake Campground Road. Travel north for approximately 15 km from Highway 3 to a dirt access road on the left. (Mount Ward is visible to the west.) Drive 2 km to a parking area. Signs there mark the trailhead. No motorized vehicles can travel beyond the trailhead as there is a deep ditch across the road.

An easy scramble takes you up to a mountain lake encircled by impressive cliffs, including those of Mount Ward. Snow remains on the scree slopes and in the sheltered areas around the lake into midsummer. The "window" in the mountain is not visible from the lake, but can be seen as you drive along the Allison Creek Road. The lake is stocked with cutthroat trout, and anglers are usually busy along the shoreline.

The first part of the trail is a continuation of the gravel logging road, which narrows to a footpath after the logged-out area. At the fork in the road follow the signed arrow to the right. The blazed footpath leads up the hillside and steeply up a low ridge. From the ridge top, enjoy the views of South Racehorse Creek valley, Crowsnest Mountain and the Seven Sisters. Now the trail descends through the woods towards the lake. On the way you will pass a small drainage pond. A green box containing a hiker's register and volunteer fisherman report is located beside the pond.

The trail ends on the shores of Window Mountain Lake. A primitive campsite can be found a few metres to the left of the T-intersection at the shoreline.

Fishing for cutthroat trout in Window Mountain Lake

Hilary-Anne Hamilton

RACEHORSE PASS

Half-day hike; easy
Length: 3.5 km (2.1 mi.) to pass
Hiking time: 1 to 1½ hours to pass
Elevation gain: 300 m (1000 ft.)
Maximum elevation: 2100 m (6900 ft.)
Map: Tornado Mountain 82 G/15
Access: Drive 16 km north on Allison Creek Road from Highway 3, keeping right at the junction with Chinook Lake Campground Road. Mileage is marked by signs. Immediately before the 10-mile sign turn left onto Racehorse Pass Road, follow it for 300 m, and park where a deep ditch crosses the road.

The impressive alpine scenery of the Racehorse Pass area makes this a superb hike. Wildflower enthusiasts especially will be kept happy for hours by the profusion of alpine blooms. With the option of scrambling some low hills near the pass, each with its own outstanding views, this area is worth a full day's exploration. Snow patches cover much of the upper section of the route into mid-June, making travel difficult.

Leave the trailhead and immediately cross two small runoff creeks. The trail then enters an enclosed forest of lodgepole pine and rises at a steady but moderate grade. The slope of the sidehill allows views of South Racehorse Creek valley and of logged-out area across the valley, and partial views of Crowsnest Mountain to the south. The High Rock Range dominates the southwestern skyline. As the trail steepens, waterfalls are visible in the canyon far below the road. The road continues onto open scree slopes, swings right (west) towards the pass, and then begins to level out. One final short climb leads to the long, flat summit of the pass. Englemann spruce, stunted pines and some junipers grow in this open area of extensive burn. The alpine terrain is only a short scramble away. A low ridge south of the pass can easily be ascended and it offers excellent views south to Crowsnest Mountain and Window Mountain Lake; Erickson Ridge can be seen on the western horizon.

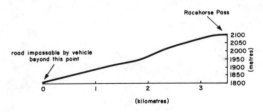

SOUTH RACEHORSE TRIBUTARY

Day hike; easy to moderate
Length: 5.5 km (3.2 mi.) to end of road
Hiking time: 3 to 4 hours to headwall at end of trail
Elevation gain: 580 m (1900 ft.)
Maximum elevation: 2250 m (7400 ft.)
Map: Tornado Mountain 82 G/15
Access: From Highway 3, drive north up Allison Creek Road for just over
19 km. The trailhead is at a rough cart track on the left (southwest).

This is for the most part, a rather uneventful hike to a mountain cirque, but
the open meadows and the view from the ridge top make it worthwhile.

The cart track runs west up the valley of a small tributary creek, through 1
km of young spruce forest. Take the left fork in the logged-out area and
continue up the main valley, passing through a forest of spruce and fir. After
the 3-km mark, the road begins a gradual ascent, then ends at the base of one
of the many unnamed peaks of the High Rock Range. Snow patches remain
amidst alpine meadows and open, flowered slopes; the pink snow associated
with snow lice is not seen until the final melt.

Continue up the headwall beyond the end of the road for the best part of
this hike. This requires a steep scramble, rising over 400 m in less than a
kilometre, and should only be undertaken by those confident of their abilities.
Take some time to explore the impressive cirque at the top of the headwall.
Views from the lip of the cirque extend far to the north.

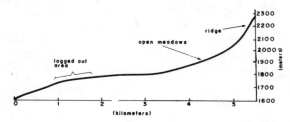

95

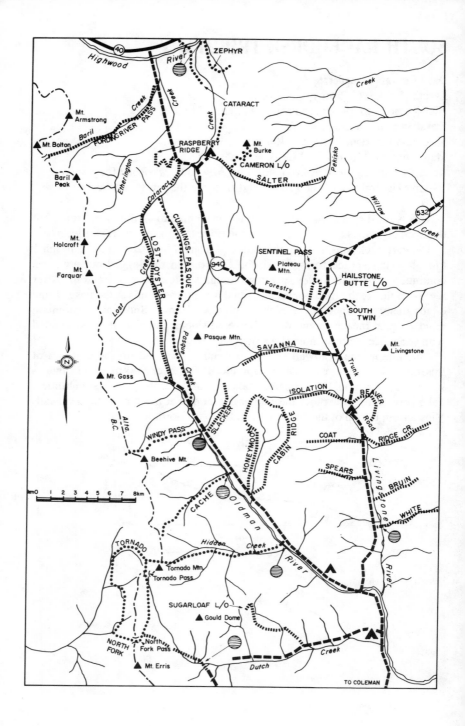

OLDMAN RIVER AREA

The Oldman River derives its name from a spot near the confluence of the Oldman and Livingstone rivers, the "Old Man's playground" of Indian folklore; the mythical "Old Man" was thought to have supernatural powers. Stone cairns, built by travellers to bring good luck, once marked the spot. The river originates in the High Rock Range and flows southeast across the Livingstone Range to the prairies, crossing the range through a unique geological feature known as the Gap. This gash in the mountain chain was probably cut originally by the river and widened and modified during glaciation. The dominant rock types of the Livingstone Range are resistant limestones and dolomites. The Oldman tributaries include, near its headwaters, Oyster, Slacker, Pasque and Cache creeks, and, farther downstream, Dutch and Racehorse creeks and the Livingstone River. The Crowsnest and Castle rivers eventually join it before it flows into the South Saskatchewan River on the prairies.

Major campgrounds include the Oldman River, Dutch Creek, Livingstone River and Racehorse Creek sites. The Forestry Trunk Road provides the main access to the area.

The view north from the headwaters of Cache Creek

HIDDEN CREEK

Backpack; difficult
Length: 14 km (8.7 mi.) to saddle
Hiking time: 8 hours to saddle
Elevation gain: 200 m (700 ft.)
Maximum elevation: 1800 m (5900 ft.)
Maps: Maycroft 82 G/16; Tornado Mountain 82 G/15
Access: Drive Oldman River Road 7.0 km west from its junction with the Forestry Trunk Road. The trail begins on the west side of the Oldman River at its confluence with Hidden Creek.

This backpacking trip leads through valley and forest to a close-up view of the impressive sheer cliffs of Tornado Mountain and Gould Dome. The hike is best reserved for late season, when water levels on the Oldman River recede. The Tornado Pass–North Fork Pass Loop trail can be reached via this trail.

"Plunge" right into this hike by fording the icy-cold Oldman River (20 m wide, thigh deep, fast-flowing) to reach the trailhead on a dirt road that leads from an outfitter's camp. Hidden Creek is heard but not seen as the road rises gently, and views open up along the valley to Tornado Mountain. Now the trail descends into the valley, alongside the creek and through poplar stands.

Head right at the fork to avoid crossing the creek again. A tributary now parallels Hidden Creek through stands of pine trees; you will cross it 4.0 km from the trailhead. When you reach the top of a knoll at the 7.0-km mark, you can take a side trip up a path on the ridge to the right for a view of Tornado Mountain. The road continues down from the knoll to an outfitter's camp, and from the surrounding meadows there are good views of Gould Dome and Tornado Mountain. To avoid a ford where the road crosses Hidden Creek, take a detour along the cut-line to the right.

At the 8.5-km mark, the creek divides and the route follows South Hidden Creek. Tornado Mountain again dominates viewpoints along the way.

Continue straight. The route eventually swings away from the creek along a cut-line ascending a low hill. You will be slowed down as you pass through a boggy area, but admiring towering Gould Dome will help you forget the sloppy ground. Cross another tributary. About 100 m before the road ends on the bank of South Hidden Creek, follow a blazed and flagged footpath west and uphill through the trees. This joins a horse trail that leads up a steep scree slope to a basin and saddle below Tornado Mountain. The headwaters of Dutch Creek and the Tornado Pass environs are just across the saddle. Some bushwhacking is required. (This section is described in the Tornado Pass–North Fork Pass trail and is for skilled route-finders only.)

TORNADO PASS–NORTH FORK PASS

Backpack; difficult
Length: 32 km (20 mi.) to complete loop
Hiking time: 2 to 3 days
Elevation gain: 400 m (1300 ft.)
Elevation loss: 550 m (1800 ft.)
Maximum elevation: 2150 m (7000 ft.)
Map: Tornado Mountain 82 G/15
Access: Drive 30.5 km north on Allison Creek Road. The road crosses both South and North Racehorse creeks, eventually arriving at a washed-out bridge on Dutch Creek. You must ford the creek to reach the trailhead on the north side.

An outstanding backpacking trip through two Continental Divide passes, this hike is a veritable wildlife safari. Bear, moose, deer, elk and mountain sheep are plentiful in this remote area, and encounters are inevitable. Tornado Pass is named for its frequent fierce storms. Hikers should be aware of this and be prepared for very sudden weather changes.

After fording Dutch Creek (15 m wide, knee to thigh deep) make your way north on a rough road paralleling the east bank of the creek. At the 5.0-km mark you reach a major intersection. The left (west) fork leads in 2 km to North Fork Pass; Tornado pass lies 6 km ahead, at the end of some rough bushwhacking; and between the two, a loop trail covers some 14 km of bushwhacking game trails and logging roads along Tornado and Line creeks in British Columbia. Although the distance is not great, much of this route is poorly defined and travel is tedious and time consuming. A topographic map is definitely required.

Continue straight up the valley towards Tornado Pass between the sheer walls of neighbouring peaks. In spring, much of the valley bottom is very soggy. Some heavy bushwhacking is required to reach the wooded pass. From there, the route descends Tornado Creek into British Columbia and swings west around a small peak. Game trails crisscross through a sparse forest of spruce and larch. Follow an exploration road from the south side of the creek through a section of rockfall, where immense boulders are strewn about.

Climb over rocks and deadfall to the end of the road, and descend steeply through heavy timber towards Tornado Creek. Cross to the creek's south side and head west along a logging road. The area has been extensively logged, but spruce trees have begun to regenerate. The creek must be crossed once again before the road swings away from it and rises to the west. Several good campsites can be found in the next few kilometres. Stay left (south) and cross Line Creek. The route continues south below Horseshoe Ridge, climbing gradually through a lodgepole pine forest. As it rises more steeply, it turns briefly west before continuing south. Wisukitsak Ridge and Mount Lyne stand out to the north.

When you reach a T-intersection, turn left (east) towards North Fork Pass, 3.5 km distant. North Fork Pass, like Tornado, is heavily forested, and views are limited. The road descends from the pass to Dutch Creek and turns right (south). The trailhead is 5 km down the road.

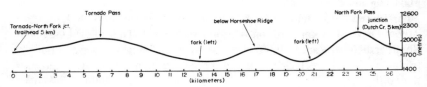

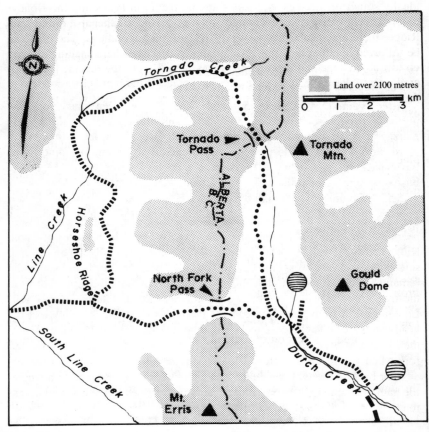

CABIN RIDGE–HONEYMOON CREEK

Day hike; easy to moderate
Length: 20.6 km (12.8 mi.) round trip (loop)
Hiking time: 5 to 7 hours
Elevation gain: 550 m (1800 ft.)
Maximum elevation: 2400 m (7900 ft.)
Map: Fording River 82 J/2
Access: Drive 13.6 km west on the Oldman River Road from the Forestry Trunk Road. Turn east onto a gas well access road. The trailhead begins on the right-hand side, 250 m down the road.

The trail, a rough cart track built during seismic exploration in the area, is ideally suited for hiking, as it loops around the Twin Peaks and the Honeymoon Creek valley and eventually returns to the trailhead. From Cabin Ridge, there are spectacular views of the surrounding valleys. The hike can be followed in either direction. Although it is described here heading directly up to Cabin Ridge and descending Honeymoon Creek, the reverse is considered a more desirable hike, as it takes advantage of the rapid elevation loss at the route's end. If you have the time and energy, you may wish to further explore seismic roads off the route. These are marked on the Fording River topographic map.

The moderately graded route leads 1.5 km east from the trailhead through a pine and spruce forest. Keep left at a fork just after the route begins to steepen. The steep ascent over the next 6 km is interrupted only by a short drop into a small valley directly above the gas well at the end of the access road. The trail emerges above the tree line at the 7.6-km mark. You can see the next section of the route as it loops ahead below Twin Peaks and disappears into the trees on the opposite side of the valley. The hillsides of Cabin Ridge across the valley appear to be grassy, but they are really lichen-covered scree slopes. To the west the High Rock Range stretches north and south and remains visible all along Cabin Ridge. At the 10-km mark the route returns to the tree line and winds north; two kilometres farther it turns sharply left. Looking north from here, you can see the upper Coat Creek valley and the headwaters of Honeymoon Creek. Continue on the road as it swings south, then switches back after 400 m and skirts the far north ridge. Take the left fork when you reach a T-intersection. The remainder of the hike is a gradual descent back to the Oldman River Road, the last 600 m reduced to a single-file path. The trail ends approximately 200 m northwest of the gas well access road.

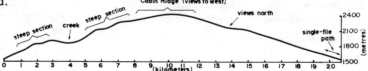

CACHE CREEK

Day hike/backpack; difficult
Length: 19 km (12 mi.) round trip
Hiking time: 7 to 10 hours
Elevation gain: 450 m (1475 ft.)
Maximum elevation: 2195 m (7200 ft.)
Maps: Tornado Mountain 82 G/15; Fording River 82 J/2
Access: From the Oldman River Campground, follow the road west for approximately 16 km to Oldman Falls. The trail starts at a rough road on the west side of the Oldman River, opposite the campground above the falls.

A small lake and superb alpine and subalpine meadows are the rewards for this difficult bushwhacking route up Cache Creek. Take note that the trail is nonexistent in the upper reaches and is only for experienced hikers.

The trail starts with a tricky ford of the Oldman River (15 m wide, knee to thigh deep, fast running) which is followed immediately by an easy ford of Cache Creek (3 m wide, ankle deep). On the south side of Cache Creek, follow a rough road into a dense lodgepole pine forest. Less than a kilometre from the Oldman River you will pass a log cabin that has seen better days. The route eventually becomes a single-file trail. As the terrain opens up into meadows, the trail stays close to the banks of Cache Creek, which you must ford three times, though the second and third fords can be avoided if you keep to the north side of the creek. The trail re-enters the forest where many game trails intersect it. Deeper into the forest, the trail becomes less well defined and at times disappears completely. Stay close to the creek; the forest cover is generally sparser on the banks. The trail continues along the valley, becoming little more than random game trails crisscrossing the valley bottom. Bushwhacking becomes a way of life at this point. Cache Creek forks approximately 5 km up from the Oldman River. Take the left fork and head up a narrow, steep valley. Much deadfall litters the moss-covered valley floor so travel is easiest at creek level; cross whenever necessary. At the next fork in the creek, stay right and continue up the narrow valley.

After a kilometre the route opens up to swampy subalpine meadows which are profuse with white globe flowers in early summer. The lake at the head of Cache Creek is little more than a pond, much smaller than the lake shown on the Fording River topographic map. The peaceful meadows around the lake are a stark contrast to the ominous grey cliffs of the High Rock Range looming overhead. Now continue south into alpine meadows and climb the rocky 2200-m pass to take in the fine views north to Tornado Mountain, south to Beehive Mountain and east to the Livingstone Range.

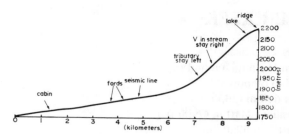

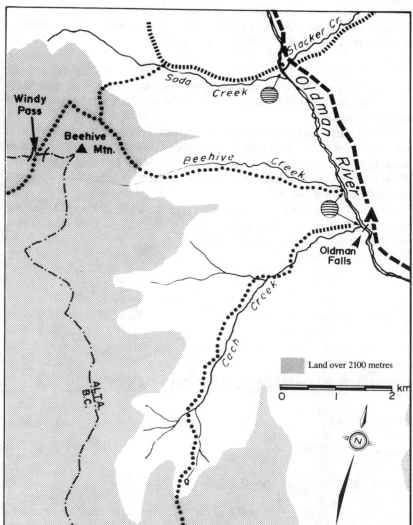

Land over 2100 metres

0   1   2 km

N

SLACKER CREEK

Day hike; easy
Length: 17 km (10.5 mi.) round trip
Hiking time: 5 to 6 hours
Elevation gain: 610 m (2000 ft.)
Maximum elevation: 2410 m (7900 ft.)
Map: Fording River 82 J/2
Access: The trailhead is located on the south side of the Slacker Creek Bridge, approximately 21 km west from the junction of the Oldman River Road and the Forestry Trunk Road (Highway 940).

This hill climb above Slacker Creek offers superb views of the Continental Divide in the west. The creek takes its name from the World War I draftdodgers or "slackers," who hid out in cabins in the area. Little remains today of the original cabins.

The trail starts out as a well-defined cart track alongside Slacker Creek; it soon turns right (east) and eventually crosses a creek tributary. The trail then returns to and crosses Slacker Creek. After a steady but moderate climb to the hilltop, the trail narrows to a single-file path which leads left (west) along a ridge to the top of a bare hill.

Below and to the west are the headwaters of the Oldman River. Above the river are, from left to right, Beehive Mountain, Mount Lyall and Mount Gass. Pasque Mountain rises directly north.

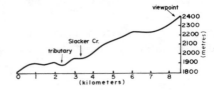

BEEHIVE MOUNTAIN–WINDY PASS

Day hike; difficult
Length: 7.2 km (4.5 mi.) to pass
Hiking time: 4 to 5 hours
Elevation gain: 700 m (2300 ft.)
Maximum elevation: 2470 (8100 ft.)
Map: Fording River 82 J/2
Access: The trail begins 50 m past Slacker Creek at an old outfitter's camp on the Oldman River Road, approximately 21 km from Oldman River Campground.

The early sections of this trail are not too interesting and there is a fair amount of elevation gain, but the varied terrain and fine views near the end make the trip well worth the effort. Colourful patches of glacier lilies grow at lower elevations in early summer, and the ridge is dotted with cinquefoil, forget-me-nots and purple fringe. Shrubby beard tongue, mountain heather and purple saxifrage appear at the upper limits of the alpine vegetation zone. Bushwhacking will be required to follow the ridge below Beehive Mountain. Options exist to climb the mountain, or to cross over Windy Pass into British Columbia.

Ford the Oldman River (10 m wide, knee deep, slow flowing) and follow a cut-line due west for almost 3 km up the west bank. Leave the cut-line where it turns sharply north and dips towards the valley bottom. You must cross the valley to reach the base of Beehive Mountain. There is no defined trail in the valley, and you will have to bushwhack or follow one of the numerous game trails which lead west through spruce and lodgepole pine. Soda Creek, which flows down the centre of the valley, is easily crossed. Aim for the ridge that juts east from the base of Beehive Mountain. The forest begins to thin at the top of the ridge; shorter, stockier trees such as larch, white pine, Englemann spruce and alpine fir are dominant. Follow game trails up to the open grassy slopes beneath scree slopes abundant with wildflowers. Little regeneration has occurred in the upper valley or along the ridges since a fire devastated this area a number of years ago.

The view from the base of Beehive Mountain takes in Mount Lyall, Mount Gass and the Oldman River. Continue towards the 2400-m elevation mark approximately 6 km from the trailhead. An old outfitter's trail winds around the northeast flank of the mountain, over steep side slopes and open scree slopes to Windy Pass.

The view from the pass is dominated by the cliffs of the High Rock Range. Good views extend west into British Columbia and east to the Oldman River valley.

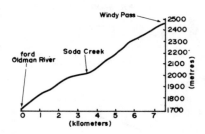

105

Beehive Creek Access

Although the Soda Creek access is shorter, Beehive Creek does provide alternative access to Beehive Mountain and Windy Pass. Ford the Oldman River and follow Beehive Creek, eventually ascending the ridge that extends southeast from Beehive Mountain. From here, follow the route described under the Beehive Mountain–Windy Pass trail.

SUGARLOAF LOOKOUT

Day hike; moderate to difficult
Length: 8 km (5 mi.) to top
Hiking time: 5 to 6 hours return
Elevation gain: 990 m (3250 ft.)
Maximum elevation: 2515 m (8250 ft.)
Maps: Maycroft 82 G/16; Tornado Mountain 82 G/15
Access: Drive the Forestry Trunk Road as far as the Dutch Creek Campground. Follow the road to the right of the campground for approximately 8 km and park at the fork.

Don't forget to pack a camera on this hike. Sugarloaf Lookout, at 2525 m, is the highest of the Bow-Crow Forest lookouts. Besides its spendid panorama, it has the added bonus of a uniquely mosaicked helicopter pad that a past attendant spent three summers creating.

From the intersection, take the right fork along a gradual uphill through mixed forest. The road steepens, and after approximately 3 km, opens up to grassy meadows. From here, Gould Dome and Tornado Mountain stand out in the south.

The road continues to climb and swings around to the north side of Sugarloaf Mountain, opening up a view east to the Porcupine Hills. The last 3 km are a constant, steep uphill, but you won't regret the climb once you see the panorama from the top.

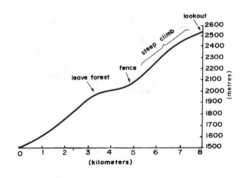

LIVINGSTONE FIRE LOOKOUT

Day hike; moderate
Length: 9.5 km (5.9 mi.) to lookout
Hiking time: 2½ to 4 hours to lookout
Elevation gain: 670 m (2225 ft.)
Maximum elevation: 2100 m (6900 ft.)
Map: Maycroft 82 G/16
Access: Drive the Forestry Trunk Road approximately 46 km north from
Coleman. The trailhead is directly opposite the turnoff to the Oldman River
Road Campground, and the route begins on a gravel road. You may choose
to drive the flat stretch of road in towards the Livingstone River Bridge; if
you do, park just across the bridge. There are few places to park beyond
here, and eventually a locked gate bars the road. A warning sign between
the bridge and the gate advises against further travel along the road by
motorized vehicles.

This four-wheel-drive road leads up to the Livingstone Fire Lookout.
Although 640 m of elevation are gained in the last 4.5 km, the numerous
switchbacks make the hike seem less difficult. There are different and more
magnificent views of mountains and valleys at every turn along the way, and
the panorama from the lookout is spectacular. The first 5 km along the gravel
road are relatively flat; the real climbing only begins after the gate.

From the lookout you can see the Front Ranges in the west, including
Tornado Mountain and Gould Dome, Livingstone Range with Mount Living-
stone and Chaffen Ridge in the north, and Thunder Mountain in the south.
The Porcupine Hills, Whaleback Ridge and the prairies are visible in the east.
(The Livingstone Range was named after David Livingstone, the noted Afri-
can explorer, by Thomas Blakiston in 1858.)

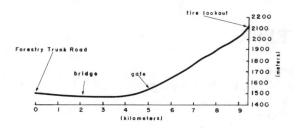

WHITE CREEK

Day hike; moderate
Length: 8 km (5 mi.) to small lake
Hiking time: 3 to 5 hours
Elevation gain: 1525 m (500 ft.)
Maximum elevation: 1670 m (5500 ft.)
Map: Maycroft 82 G/16
Access: Drive north on the Forestry Trunk Road 4 km past the Oldman River Campground turnoff and turn east onto a rough cart track leading through a field. Follow this track for 200 m and park just before it descends into the Livingstone River valley.

   White Creek is a very pleasant hike through a classic example of ranchland. You are well advised to take along a pair of running shoes because your feet are bound to get wet; the route crosses White Creek and its tributaries no fewer than five times.

   Ford the Livingstone River (10 m wide, knee deep) below the parking area and follow the road straight ahead and up a hill. Leading through a mixed forest of spruce, fir, aspen and poplar, the road turns north and then east and parallels the river's south bank. It first crosses White Creek at the 2.8-km mark, and enters the more open, grassy terrain on the north side of the creek.

   Now the route leads up the valley, occasionally crossing the creek or one of its tributaries. Take the right fork at the 7-km mark and head up the wide valley through 1 km of open fields. After a short forested section, the route emerges beside a spring-fed beaver pond. The road on the east side of the pond leads farther south. Mixed forest and grassland cover the surrounding hills with some rock outcroppings on the slopes.

   An option exists to explore farther down the road, which eventually leads to Jackknife Coulee.

BRUIN CREEK

Day hike; moderate
Length: 6.4 km (4 mi.) to Chaffen Ridge
Hiking time: 2 to 3 hours to ridge
Elevation gain: 655 m (2148 ft.)
Maximum elevation: 2225 m (7298 ft.)
Map: Langford Creek 82 J/1
Access: From Highway 532, drive approximately 19.3 km south on the Forestry Trunk Road. The trail starts on the east side of the road.

At the head of Bruin Creek, Chaffen Ridge provides fine views of the immediate surroundings and makes a great ridge walk for hikers with the time and energy. Take note that the Langford Creek topographic map does not indicate a trail on Bruin Creek.

The trail fords the Livingstone River after half a kilometre (15 m wide, knee deep). Follow the trail along the south bank of Bruin Creek, straight and uphill. Just ahead of where the road ends, an easy scramble will lead you across a rocky slope to the top of Chaffen Ridge.

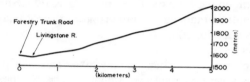

SPEARS CREEK

Half-day hike; easy
Length: 5 km (3.2 mi.) to end of road
Hiking time: 2 to 3 hours
Elevation gain: 245 m (800 ft.)
Maximum elevation: 1860 m (6100 ft.)
Map: Langford Creek 82 J/1
Access: From Highway 532, drive south on the Forestry Trunk Road for 16 km. Park in a clearing approximately 100 m down an old logging road on the west side of the Forestry Trunk Road.

The trail heads west from the clearing through a lodgepole pine forest. Although there is little outstanding scenery en route, the pines are pleasant company on a sunny day. The route generally parallels Spears Creek, crossing it at the 1.5-, 4.1- and 4.6-km marks. Crossings are simple and can be done with a little rock-hopping. Around the 3.8-km mark the route becomes soft and swampy, but the wet area extends only 30 m and is easily skirted. The trail end is approximately 400 m beyond the last creek crossing, over a small hill. A poorly defined single-file game trail continues up Spears Creek beyond the end of the road, remaining in the forested valley bottom much of the way.

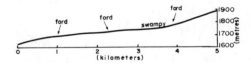

COAT CREEK

Day hike; moderate
Length: 6 km (3.7 mi.) to viewpoint
Hiking time: 1½ to 2½ hours to viewpoint
Elevation gain: 425 m (1400 ft.)
Maximum elevation: 2070 m (6800 ft.)
Maps: Langford Creek 82 J/1; Fording River 82 J/2
Access: Drive 12.5 km south on the Forestry Trunk Road from Highway 532. Park at the side of the road at a turnoff heading west onto a rough seismic road.

The Coat Creek trail is a rather ordinary hike. The lodgepole pine forest restricts views until the 6-km mark, but the hike is ideal for those who enjoy a quiet forest walk. Options exist to bushwhack past the trail's end to join either the Cabin Ridge or the Isolation Creek trail.

The rough, rocky seismic road immediately enters a lodgepole pine forest, and after 100 m crosses an underground gas pipeline. Continue along the road up the side of Coat Creek valley, staying well above creek level. You will come to several long steep sections, and a few small runoff streams along the way are easily crossed. At the 6-km mark, near the 2100-m level, the route emerges from the forest cover, affording open views to the west. Cabin Ridge stands as a prominent landmark across Coat Creek valley. Unless you plan to hike the Cabin Ridge–Honeymoon Creek trail or the Isolation Creek trail, there is little point in continuing farther. For either option, route-finding experience and a topographic map are needed, and some heavy bushwhacking will be required.

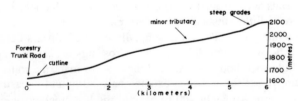

RIDGE CREEK

Half-day hike; easy
Length: 16 km (10 mi.) round trip
Hiking time: 3 to 4 hours
Elevation gain: 215 m (700 ft.)
Maximum elevation: 1765 m (5800 ft.)
Map: Langford Creek 82 J/1
Access: The trail starts approximately 1.5 km south of the Livingstone Falls Campground on the Forestry Trunk Road. The trailhead is on the east side of the road, 200 m before the Livingstone River Bridge.

This is an easy outing that leads into some beautiful ranchland, and it is an excellent half-day hike if you are camping at Livingstone Falls. Because this is ranching country, be sure to close all gates behind you.

The trail is a well-defined cart track, and begins by running parallel to the Livingstone River. It then cuts left, climbs gently through a forest of trembling aspen into the open fields of Ridge Creek valley, and ends at the base of Horseshoe Ridge.

Beehive Mountain seen from Cummings-Pasque Ridge

Hilary-Anne Hamilton

111

BEAVER CREEK CIRCUIT

Half-day hike; easy
Length: 6.3 km (3.9 mi.) one way
Hiking time: 1½ to 2½ hours
Elevation gain: 150 m (500 ft.)
Maximum elevation: 1900 m (6300 ft.)
Map: Langford Creek 82 J/1
Access: The trail is a gravel road beginning 1.3 km north of Livingstone
Falls Campground, and it ends on the Forestry Trunk Road 1 km south of
Livingstone Falls.

The Blackfoot Indians named this the creek "where the beaver cuts
wood." The circuit is easy, very short and has no major elevation gain, and is
therefore suited for beginners, people with children or anyone wishing a
casual walk. This hike is best saved for late July and August when the many
raspberry bushes and strawberry plants near the trail end bear fruit. For those
climbing Mount Livingstone, the trail can be used as an access to its base.

Follow the gravel road on its gentle climb through the forest. After about 1
km, the trees thin and the trail opens onto rolling fields sparsely populated
with wildflowers. Mount Livingstone can be seen in the east. The route then
turns south and forks into three; take the middle (east) fork. Near the fork a
dry creek bed, which at one time was Beaver Creek, is now barely distinguishable from the surrounding terrain. From the creek bed the trail heads up
to the top of a hill, where the views include the High Rock Range in the west.
The trail gradually loses elevation and turns west, hugging the side of a ridge.
Trees flank the trail on the right and open fields on the left. In the last
kilometre the trail again enters the forest. Wild raspberry bushes and
strawberry plants grow abundantly alongside the road.

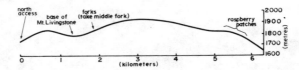

112

ISOLATION CREEK RIDGE

Day hike; moderate
Length: 15 km (9.3 mi.) to ridge top
Hiking time: 4 to 5 hours
Elevation gain: 850 m (2770 ft.)
Elevation loss: 150m (500 ft.)
Maximum elevation: 2550 m (8372 ft.)
Maps: Langford Creek 82 J/1; Fording River 82 J/2
Access: The trailhead is found on the west side of the Forestry Trunk Road
(Highway 940), 2.3 km north of Livingstone Falls.

This is a ridge hike like few others. It passes through open fields and along
a forested valley and ends with spectacular views from the top of Isolation
Creek Ridge. The hike can be made longer by connecting it with other trails,
such as Savanna Creek, Honeymoon Creek and Cabin Ridge.

Follow the trail across a large field, and ford the Livingstone River, which
is divided here into two channels (each 5 m wide, ankle to calf deep). The
trail ascends the valley, at first climbing gently. Pass several minor roads
branching off the main trail; the first major intersection is not reached until
the 8.1-km mark. Take the left fork to Isolation Creek Ridge. (The right fork
leads to the Savanna Creek trail with an option to head up to Twin Peaks on
Cabin Ridge and Honeymoon Creek.) The road descends to another major
intersection where you must keep to the right before climbing the steep west
side of the ridge. From the ridge top, several recognizable peaks can be
identified in the High Rock Range, including Beehive and Lyall mountains.
Pasque Mountain is in the foreground and Isola Peak is to the east.

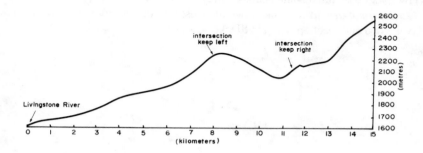

113

SAVANNA CREEK

Day hike; moderate
Length: 9.5 km (6 mi.) one way
Hiking time: 5 to 6 hours round trip
Elevation gain: 490 m (1600 ft.)
Maximum elevation: 2350 m (7700 ft.)
Maps: Langford Creek 82 J/1; Fording River 82 J/2
Note: Take along running shoes for the many fords. There is no water past
the last creek crossing, so fill your water bottle before climbing the ridge.
Access: Drive north on the Forestry Trunk Road just over 6 km from the
Livingstone Falls Campground. Turn left on a gas well access road. Ignore
the first fork to the left; the trail starts at the second fork to the left,
approximately 3 km from the Forestry Trunk Road.

This trail leads up the Savanna Creek valley to the top of a ridge where
there are excellent views east and west.

From the trailhead, the route drops about 30 m into the forested valley of
spruce and fir. The valley soon flattens out and you will ford Savanna Creek
half a dozen times. After 6 km the creek moves away from the trail, and you
begin a gradual ascent towards the ridge, passing by an outfitter's camp along
the way. The route gradually narrows to a single-file path along what looks
like an overgrown cut-line. It curves to the right and after about 3 km arrives
at the top of the ridge. The terrain here is open and treeless and many
wildflowers grow in the grassy cover: forget-me-nots, cinquefoil and purple
saxifrage are the most prominent. The impressive view includes the Oldman
River valley and the High Rock Range in the west, and you also have a good
view back down the Savanna Creek valley.

An option exists to continue down the west side of the ridge to the Oldman
River Road and meet up with the Slacker Creek trail.

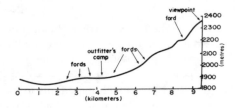

SOUTH TWIN CREEK

Half-day hike; easy
Length: 4 km (2.4 mi.) return
Hiking time: 3 to 4 hours return
Elevation gain: 180 m (600 ft.)
Maximum elevation: 2000 m (6550 ft.)
Map: Langford Creek 82 J/1
Access: Drive approximately 1 km south on the Forestry Trunk Road from Highway 532. The trail leads east from the Forestry Trunk Road, just north of a cattle guard on a seismic road.

South Twin Creek trail can be extended to include ridges that offer fine views in all directions. If you have the time and energy, you can make a short side trip to a small lake.

The trail climbs gradually through a fir and spruce forest for 1 km and then opens into meadows where you will ford a small creek. Continue along the trail as it wanders between tree patches and meadow before swinging east towards a saddle between two ridges. Climb up the ridge to the right for a view east to the Porcupine Hills, north to Hailstone Butte, and west to the Tornado Mountain area. The adventuresome can hike up to the small lake on the ridge to the north.

HAILSTONE BUTTE FIRE LOOKOUT

Half-day hike; easy
Length: 9.3 km (5.8 mi.) to lookout
Hiking time: 3 to 5 hours
Elevation gain: 500 m (1650 ft.)
Maximum elevation: 2360 m (7750 ft.)
Map: Langford Creek 82 J/1
Access: Drive 100 m west on the Forestry Trunk Road from Highway 532. Take the gravel access road north for 200 m and park at the restricted access gate. The route heads north from the other side of the gate.

At the end of this trip there is, as with most trails to lookout stations, an excellent panorama of the surrounding area, so don't forget to take along a camera. Like other lookouts in the Bow-Crow Forest, Hailstone Butte is manned from April to October, and visits with the attendants are informative and enjoyable.

For the first 5.1 km beyond the gate, the road leads through a lodgepole pine and spruce forest and parallels a small creek part of the way. In a large clearing 2 km from the trailhead, you can see the lookout on the ridge to the right (east).

Keep right at both forks on the access road, at the 3.9-km and 5.1-km marks. After the second fork the road becomes a rough track that skirts the north end of Hailstone Butte and ascends the east flank of the ridge to the lookout. As the grade steepens, the road switchbacks to the summit. Strong winds frequently gust across the top of the exposed ridge on the last stretch of the road. The lookout, 0.5 km farther south along the butte, is an excellent vantage point: views extend as far south as Chief Mountain on the U.S. border; the Crowsnest Pass area, nearby Livingstone and Tornado mountains, and Gould Dome are also visible, and on a clear day Calgary can be seen in the northwest.

For a time-saving alternative approach to the lookout, turn east onto Highway 532 from the Forestry Trunk Road and drive for 3.8 km to a small lake on the right-hand (east) side of the road. Although route-finding is required, the area is very open, and the lookout remains in plain view at all times. You will have to scramble 335 m up the grass and rock slope of the Hailstone Butte, but the open surroundings make this a desirable route, and the overall distance is much shorter.

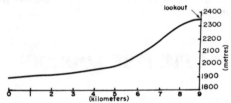

SENTINEL PASS

Day hike; easy
Length: 8.6 km (5.3 mi.) to Sentinel Pass
Hiking time: 2 to 3 hours
Elevation gain: 280 m (920 ft.)
Maximum elevation: 2125 m (6980 ft.)
Map: Langford Creek 82 J/1
Access: Drive 100 m west on the Forestry Trunk Road from Highway 532. Take the gravel access road 200 m north and park at the restricted access gate.

Sentinel Pass is a broad, expansive 2125-m-high pass below the unique geological formations of Plateau Mountain and Sentinel Peak. An option is a short side trip to a rocky col where there are good views east across the prairies.

The first 5.8 km past the gate are a road walk through an open forest of spruce and pine. The forest and terrain limit the views, but at the 2-km mark Hailstone Butte Fire Lookout is visible on the exposed ridge on the right (east). Head right when the road forks after 3.9 km. Another right fork after 1.2 km onto a rough and rocky road eventually leads to Hailstone Butte Lookout. Continue on the fire lookout road until, 0.7 km from the last fork, it swings back directly south. From here, turn into a dry valley that joins the road from the north; it opens up into grassy meadows after 300 m, and you can follow cow trails along the valley bottom. An obvious col is visible north up the valley and the trail leads to its base, 1.3 km from the lookout road. Take the easiest route through the sparse forest up to the col, but be prepared for the strong winds that often whip through the exposed gap. The expansive views east take in much of the farming country in the Nanton area. Sentinel Pass is visible as sparsely treed meadow, only 1.5 km northwest.

Return to the valley bottom, where the route swings west as it passes through a spruce and lodgepole pine forest, then opens up to a steady but moderate climb over the last half-kilometre to Sentinel Pass. The pass, 1 km wide and over 2100 m in elevation, allows good views in all directions. Only low brush and a few Englemann spruce grow here. Explore the area; you can also take a short jaunt to the ridge adjoining Sentinel Peak.

Return along the same route, or follow a seismic line on the west side of the main valley that leads directly back through a lodgepole pine forest to a point only 300 m from the Hailstone Butte Lookout Road.

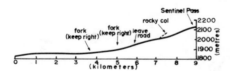

CAMERON LOOKOUT

Day hike; moderate
Length: 8 km (5 mi.) to lookout
Hiking time: 4 to 6 hours return
Elevation gain: 850 m (2800 ft.)
Maximum elevation: 2540 m (8300 ft.)
Map: Mount Head 82 J/7
Access: From the Forestry Trunk Road, drive into the overnight camping area of Cataract Creek Campground and park approximately 100 m south of the Salter Creek bridge.

This hike climbs a heart-pounding 850 m to an abandoned fire lookout on the summit of Mount Burke.

From the trailhead follow the rough road that parallels Salter Creek through a forest of trembling aspens. Fill your canteens where the trail crosses Plateau Creek; there is no other water supply on this trail. Approximately 1 km from the creek a sign indicates the trail to Mount Burke. The route may be difficult to locate; though well-defined, the trail's first half-kilometre leads in the wrong direction, but soon begins to switchback through a predominantly lodgepole pine forest and emerges at the tree line on Mount Burke. Continue up a grassy slope and across a steep rocky ridge to the lookout. Be careful along the ridge; it is very narrow in places and extremely windy.

Cameron Lookout, built in 1929, once had the distinction of being, at 2540 m, the highest lookout in Canada. It was replaced in 1953 by the Raspberry Fire Lookout west across the valley. Set at such a high and exposed spot, Cameron Lookout was renowned for hair-raising excitement during lightning storms. In the mid-1930s, during one particularly spectacular storm, a young fire attendant was so unnerved by the close strikes that he pulled on only his long underwear and boots and bolted down the mountainside at full gallop. The next morning, he was found wandering in fields around Pekisko. Needless to say he never returned to his job atop Mount Burke.

Although the lookout is in poor condition, it does offer welcome relief from the wind. Directly west of the lookout is Raspberry Ridge; Baril Peak and the rounded mass of Plateau Mountain are visible to the south, and an outstanding panorama stretches westward onto the foothills and out to the prairies.

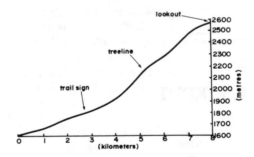

SALTER CREEK

Day hike; easy
Length: 6.7 km (4.2 mi.) to pass
Hiking time: 1½ to 2½ hours
Elevation gain: 245 m (800 ft.)
Maximum elevation: 1920 m (6300 ft.)
Maps: Mount Head 82 J/7; Stimson Creek 82 J/8
Access: From Highwood Junction drive 13 km south on the Forestry Trunk Road to Cataract Creek Campground. Follow the road into the camping area for approximately 0.7 km to the Salter Creek bridge and park on the roadside. The trail heads up on the right (south) bank of the creek.

This hike follows the course of Salter Creek to its headwaters in a pass between Mount Burke and Plateau Mountain. The route can be continued over the pass, descending from the Forest Reserve into ranchland along Pekisko Creek. Keep an eye open for interesting geological formations on surrounding mountains.

Although the road actually begins on the north side of the Salter Creek bridge, you should start on the south bank, catching the road 200 m ahead and thereby avoiding one crossing of the creek. Continue on the road up the south side of the creek and cross tiny Plateau Creek. The road then heads west up the narrow valley and crosses Salter Creek several times.

The junction with Mount Burke trail is 2.5 km from the trailhead. A sign on a tree indicates the trail up to Cameron Lookout. Stay on the road; the route gently climbs for approximately 3 km and steepens in the last kilometre to the wooded pass.

From just below the pass there is a good viewpoint of Sentinel Peak. Follow the winding road for 1 km to an open meadow with good views to the east. The road continues to the Forest Reserve boundary and beyond on a snowmobile route to Willow Creek Recreational Area.

To return, retrace your path, or scramble the avalanche slope north of the pass. Although hard work in places, this loop is very rewarding. Work through the trees along the top of the ridge to emerge at the base of a scree slope. Scramble the scree to a high point on the ridge and Mount Burke. From here, there are fine views of the foothills and open prairie to the north and east, Sentinel Peak and Plateau Mountain to the south and Mount Armstrong and Raspberry Ridge to the west. On a clear day, and with binoculars, it is possible to see Calgary to the northeast. Descend by following the large gully down to Salter Creek Road.

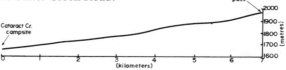

OYSTER AND LOST CREEKS

Backpack; easy
Length: 23 km (14.3 mi.), Cataract Creek to Oldman River
Hiking time: 2 days
Elevation gain: 335 m (1100 ft.)
Maximum elevation: 2040 m (6700 ft.)
Maps: Mount Head 82 J/7; Fording River J/2
Note: Arrange transportation beforehand, as it is a long 28-km hike to the
Forestry Trunk Road along the Oldman River Road.
Access: (North) The trail begins on the left side of the Forestry Trunk Road a
little less than 2 km north of Cataract Creek Campground. (South) Drive
approximately 28 km down the Oldman River Road from the Oldman River
Campground.

This perfect hike for novice backpackers leads through forests, meadows
and over rolling hills in the Lost and Oyster creek valleys. When hiking in the
spring you will come across numerous fords, and a few swampy areas will
have to be skirted.

The first few kilometres of the trail follow Cataract Creek valley through
open meadows scattered with trembling aspens. Near the end of these fields
you will pass an abandoned sawmill. Keep left at the first major fork in the
road. The trail, marked with orange triangles, leads into the trees and gains
elevation. Eventually the trail levels off and enters another open field, where
meandering Lost Creek must be forded several times. Now follow the trail
into the trees and away from Lost Creek, and climb a small ridge. The thick
forest cover prevents good views. The trail breaks over the crest of the ridge
and meets several small south-flowing tributaries of Oyster Creek. This is a
good spot for overnight camping, as it is picturesque, has water nearby and is
on dry ground. The trail follows Oyster Creek down the valley towards the
Oldman River. As it gradually loses elevation, there are sections where the
road seemingly disappears into bogs, but there is usually a path around these
swampy areas. The trail ends at the Oldman River Road.

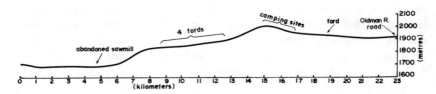

CUMMINGS–PASQUE RIDGE

Day hike/backpack; difficult
Length: 24 km (15 mi.), Cataract Creek to Oldman River
Hiking time: 8 to 10 hours
Elevation gain: 640 m (2100 ft.)
Elevation loss: 500 m (1600 ft.)
Maximum elevation: 2315 m (7600 ft.)
Maps: Mount Head 82 J/7; Fording River 82 J/2
Access: (North) The trail heads west from the Forestry Trunk Road (Highway 40) approximately 2 km north of Cataract Creek Campground. A locked gate prevents vehicle access. (South) This access is difficult to find. The trail heads north up to Pasque Ridge from the Oldman River Road approximately 24 km from the Forestry Trunk Road. Be on the lookout for a steep trail in the trees on the right-hand side of the road.

Pasque Ridge, which separates two river valleys, is the destination of this overnight hike. The trail continues along the ridge parallel to the Front Ranges of the Rockies.

If you are coming from the North Access, follow the Cataract Creek Road past an abandoned and barely recognizable mill site until you cross the third bridge over Cataract Creek. Then turn left at the T-intersection onto a logged-out cut-line marked as a snowmobile route. At the next T-intersection take the left fork, turn the corner and then take the first right down a grassy logged-out route along a stream. The route becomes ill defined at one point, but continue on over the deadfall to the cut-line in the trees. Turn onto a well-worn game trail leading from the cut-line. When it begins to turn right, look for another cut-line on the left which heads up towards the ridge. The trail may be hidden by marshy ground and deadfall, but soon becomes obvious and leads straight up to and along the ridge.

At 2300 m, the summit is the midpoint of the ridge, and is indicated by a small exposed hill protected only by a few dwarf spruce trees. From this vantage point you have a magnificent panorama in all directions: Pasque Mountain rises to the east and to the west are the Front Ranges of the Rockies. Finding a good tent site near the summit of the ridge may be difficult, but it is well worth the effort. Water may also be difficult to obtain, and it is wise to carry extra.

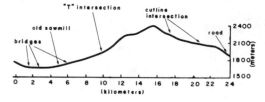

121

The trail descends gradually from the ridge, though there will be a few short climbs. Two cut-lines cut across the route. After one final descent the trail emerges on the Oldman River Road. The road is driveable for most of the hiking season, making drop-offs and pick-ups an easy arrangement.

RASPBERRY RIDGE FIRE LOOKOUT

Half-day hike; moderate
Length: 6.5 km (4 mi.) to lookout
Hiking time: 2 to 3 hours
Elevation gain: 670 m (2200 ft.)
Maximum elevation: 2350 m (7700 ft.)
Map: Mount Head 82 J/7
Note: Be sure to carry drinking water as there are no rivers or streams along the way. You might also take along a sweater or jacket; it can be quite windy on the summit.
Access: Drive the Forestry Trunk Road (Highway 940) approximately 15 km south from Highwood Junction to Cataract Creek Road, 2 km north of the Cataract Creek Campground. Turn west onto Cataract Creek Road. Park soon after the turnoff, as a steel gate farther along the trail prevents vehicle access. The trail begins on the right side of Cataract Creek Road.

This hike takes you along a hairpin road winding up to the Raspberry Ridge Fire Lookout and provides a change in scenery at every corner. The spectacular view at the top is the reward for the hard work required to get there.

The road climbs gently for the entire distance. At points along the way, it has been cut into the hillside, exposing coal seams. Surrounding mountains and river valleys can be seen from the open slopes at higher elevations, and when the trail emerges from the forest near the summit there is a view of Raspberry Ridge to the west. A full panoramic view is not possible, however, until you reach the lookout at the top. The scenery includes views of

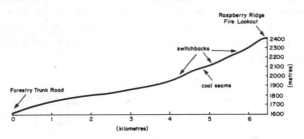

Crowsnest Mountain and the Seven Sisters to the south and the Kananaskis country to the north. Fording River Pass, the Highwood Range and Plateau Mountain are prominent landmarks in the north and west. On a clear day, and with binoculars, it is possible to see Calgary in the east.

From April to September an attendant is on duty at the lookout.

FORDING RIVER PASS

Day hike/backpack; moderate
Length: 13 km (8 mi.) to pass
Hiking time: 4 to 5 hours
Elevation gain: 730 m (2400 ft.)
Maximum elevation: 2350 m (7700 ft.)
Map: Mount Head 82 J/7
Access: The trail head is in a parking lot on the west side of the Forestry Trunk Road immediately north of Baril Creek bridge. There is a large gravel pit on the opposite side of the road.

Alpine lakes and beautiful alpine scenery make this perhaps the most spectacular hike in the entire region. Strong hikers can complete a return trip in one day, but the hike is best undertaken as a backpack with one or two nights spent in the pass. Several mountains near the pass can readily be scrambled, and exploring the pass itself will easily fill a day.

The route begins on a restricted access road leading west from the parking area. At the first fork swing left onto a single-file path down to Baril Creek. After crossing the creek on the remains of an old wooden bridge, follow the route as it joins a road heading west up the creek's south bank. You will pass through an open meadow where Baril Peak and Mount Cornwall can be seen to the west. Continue on the main road, avoiding the numerous forks. As the road passes through a burned-out area, Mount Armstrong comes into view straight ahead. The road continues through a forest of lodgepole pine, eventually reaching an area of heavy pine beetle infestation. You must cross Baril Creek once again on a sturdy bridge. Now the road heads uphill. Take the left fork; views open up of the upper Baril Creek valley and Fording Pass environs. Take another left fork; the blue blazes on trees are the work of the Great Divide Trail Association. Baril Creek flows onto the road for a short section. You should remain on the right-hand (north) side of the creek to avoid extra crossings. Follow markers through an old mill site, again staying on the north side of the creek. Shortly after the mill site, take the left (lower) fork. The creek is again crossed on a bridge. After a short uphill and a quick descent, you must cross the creek, for the fourth time, on a series of fallen logs. As the trail again ascends the valley on the north side of the creek, you will be able to see a small lake through the trees to the left. A short side trail leads to this lake.

The route continues to the seismic road and climbs steeply past the lake, with good viewpoints opening up to the west. You will encounter some large deadfall on the climb. Take the uphill (right) fork onto the steepest portion of the hike. As the road levels out at the end of the long hill, the vegetation begins to thin out, allowing fine views to the west. Continue on the seismic road towards the pass until you cross Baril Creek for the last time. There is a primitive campsite at the creek, and it is advisable that you camp here rather than in the fragile pass environment.

From Baril Creek the road continues a little more than 1 km to the pass summit. The pass is within the alpine vegetation zone, and a myriad of wildflowers bloom throughout the summer months. Several small alpine lakes dot the landscape near the summit. Numerous mountains are easily scrambled from the pass; Mount Bolton is the most accessible, and the panorama from its 2700-m summit is awe-inspiring.

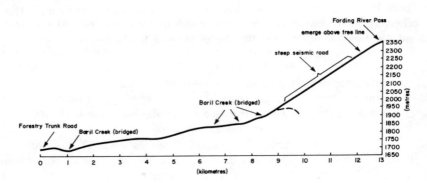

UPPER CATARACT CREEK

Half-day hike; easy to moderate
Length: 6.5 km (4 mi.) to falls
Hiking time: 1 to 1½ hours to falls
Elevation loss: 100 m (300 ft.)
Maximum elevation: 1680 m (5500 ft.)
Map: Mount Head 82 J/7
Access: Drive the Forestry Trunk Road approximately 15 km south from
Highwood Junction to Cataract Creek Campground. The trail begins at
Campsite #27. A locked steel gate prevents vehicle access.

This hike leads along Upper Cataract Creek as far as the falls, and is an
enjoyable way to spend half a day. The route begins on a cart track which is
later replaced by a well-worn game trail. At one point several trails converge
and the route is difficult to follow. The best thing to do is head as straight as
possible through the brush, and before long before you will pick up the trail
again. If you have problems, keep close to the creek until you find a trail. The
relatively small amount of water in Cataract Creek is surprisingly powerful
and over time has made some deep impressions on the landscape.

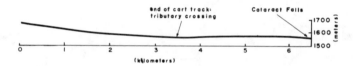

Alpine meadows near Fording River Pass

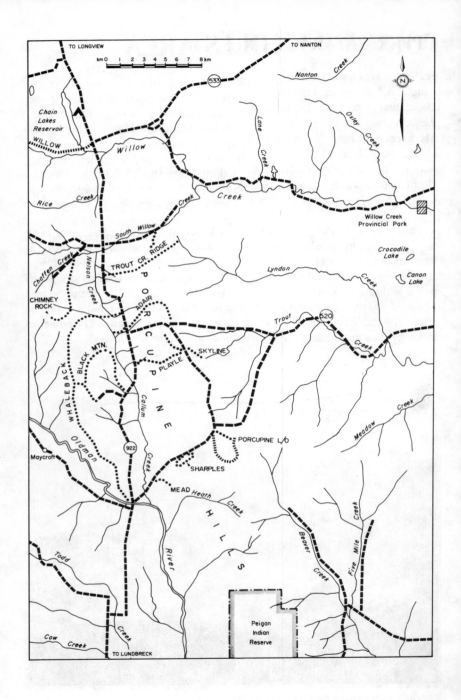

PORCUPINE HILLS AREA

The Porcupine Hills derive their name from the Blackfoot word "ky-es-kaghp-ogh-suy-is" meaning "porcupine tail," and referring to one of the hills whose shape resembles that spiny animal. By a quirk of geological fate, during the Pleistocene age, the continental ice sheet flowed around the Porcupine area, leaving a group of hills rising independently from the surrounding prairie. Ancient glacial outwash channels separated the Porcupines from the foothills; the resulting Happy Valley is occupied by the Chain Lakes, Swanson and Callum creeks and the Oldman River.

The hiking season in the Porcupine Hills begins early, as the elevation is moderate and the climate fairly dry. Maycroft Campground, Indian Grove Campground and Chain Lakes Provincial Park offer local campsites, and are accessible from Highway 22 (922).

The Rockies seen from the crest of Whaleback Ridge

MEAD CREEK RIDGE

Half-day hike; easy
Length: 1 km (0.6 mi.) to top of ridge
Hiking time: ½ to 1 hour
Elevation gain: 130 m (425 ft.)
Maximum elevation: 1525 m (4950 ft.)
Map: Maycroft 82 G/16

Access: The hike begins at Sharples Creek Road, either 8 km northeast from Highway 22 at the Oldman River bridge or 7 km southwest from the Skyline Road. Park on the shoulder at the cattle guard.

Mead Creek Ridge is a short hike which offers a fine view of the Happy Valley area. On especially sunny days, many hawks and falcons, riding the warm air currents that rise from the valley, can be seen searching for prey in the fields below.

Follow the fence line uphill from the cattle guard. The first few hundred metres cover open grassland, and then the trail enters a forest of limber pine, juniper and large Douglas-fir. Continue uphill and east until you emerge on a grassy knoll. From this, the end of the hike, there are extensive views in all directions. To the south a small ranch is nestled in the quiet Mead Creek valley. The bulk of the Porcupine Hills stands out as a forested ridge to the east. On the Whaleback Ridge to the west, an unusual vegetation feature can be observed: coniferous trees grow only on north-facing slopes of the numerous coulees, creating an impression of heavy shadows. Beyond the Whaleback rises the rugged form of the Livingstone Range, usually snow-covered until late May or early June. When the haze is not too heavy, the Flathead Range and Crowsnest Mountain are visible many miles to the southwest. The Oldman River valley is 8 km southwest and appears as a deep scar across the otherwise flat, wide bottom of Happy Valley.

SHARPLES CREEK BEAVER PONDS

Half-day hike; easy
Length: 0.5 to 1 km (0.3 to 0.6 mi.)
Hiking time: 20 minutes to 1 hour
Elevation gain: none
Maximum elevation: 1445 m (4750 ft.)
Map: Maycroft 82 G/16
Access: Approximately 750 m north of the former Skyline Ranger Station site, turn south from Skyline Road onto Sharples Creek Road. Descend for approximately 2 km; the beaver ponds are on the south side of the road. For

an alternative access from Highway 922, head north and take the first right (west) after crossing the Oldman River, approximately 24 km north of Lundbreck. Follow this unnamed road, taking two left forks, one near the 3-km mark and a second 1.5 km beyond.

The beaver ponds are obvious from anywhere along Sharples Creek Road in the valley. Park beside the creek and explore. For a pleasant outing, follow the main creek up or downstream and note the variety of wildlife and vegetation.

PORCUPINE (SKYLINE) FIRE LOOKOUT

Half-day hike; easy
Length: 1 km (0.6 mi.) to lookout
Hiking time: 1 to 2 hours return
Elevation gain: 170 m (550 ft.)
Maximum elevation: 1830 m (6000 ft.)
Map: Maycroft 82 G/16
Access: There are two possible access routes. Drive south on Highway 22, turn east onto Highway 540 for 3 km, and then south onto Skyline Road for approximately 13 km. Or, drive north on Highway 22, turn onto Sharples Creek Road approximately 300 m after crossing the Oldman River and follow it for about 19 km. Park at the junction of Skyline, Beaver Creek and Heath Creek roads, at the former site of the Skyline Ranger Station where a small white building still stands.

This trail leads to one of the highest points in the Porcupine Hills, at an elevation of 1830 m. From this lofty point, an incredible panorama stretches out to the west.

Hike east from the ranger station for 30 m to a cattle guard, where a well-defined cut-line heads north up a steep hill. Begin on the west side of the cattle guard to avoid crossing a fence later on. The cut-line passes through an enclosed forest of lodgepole, white bark and limber pine, and Douglas-fir.

An attendant is on duty at the lookout from April until the first winter snowfall. The summit although treed, is very windy, catching the westerlies head-on. In the early season, the stark whiteness of the snowbound Rockies gives an impression of impregnability, a sight that must have awed the first explorers as it awes visitors to this day. Far to the west stand the High Rock and Livingstone ranges; Whaleback Ridge and Happy Valley are in the foreground; the Elk Range is visible far to the north, the Crowsnest Pass area to the south. The mountain to the west with horizontal strata is Gould Dome, and Tornado Mountain is just north of it, rising 200 m higher.

BLACK MOUNTAIN

Half-day hike; easy
Length: 7 km (4.3 mi.) for circuit
of mountain
Hiking time: 2 to 2½ hours
Elevation gain: 465 m (1525 ft.)
Maximum elevation: 2050 m (6725 ft.)
Map: Maycroft 82 G/16
Note: Water is scarce on this hike, so fill your canteen before setting out.
Also, when passing through rangeland, be sure to close any gates you open.
Access: Drive Highway 22, 22 km south of Chain Lakes Provincial Park.
Drive past Burton Creek and continue south for 1.5 km. Black Mountain is
clearly visible about 1.5 km west of the highway. A dirt road leads west for
2 km and joins the main highway from a gap at the southern end of Black
Mountain. Park where convenient.

This pleasant circuit climbs the west ridge line, descends the east and
returns to the starting point at the south end of the hill. The terrain is largely
grass slopes, thinly wooded in parts with stands of limber pines and spruce.
Because of the openness of the area, there are views in all directions. In the
west are the north end of Whaleback Ridge and the Livingstone Range. To
the east are the Callum Creek rangelands and the Porcupine Hills.

Depending upon your time and energy, you can lengthen or shorten the
circuit, but the recommended starting point is at the south end of the mountain on the dirt road. Climb the ridge to the top and continue to an open
grassy area on the north slope. Now turn east, finding the easiest route down
to the Callum Creek valley and returning along the four-wheel-drive road that
passes through range and pastures at the mountain's base and eventually
meets the access road near the starting point.

SKYLINE (WALDRON)

Half-day hike; easy
Length: 1 km to viewpoint
Hiking time: ½ to 1 hour
Elevation gain: 90 m (300 ft.)
Maximum elevation: 1840 m (6000 ft.)
Map: Maycroft 82 G/16

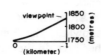

Access: Drive 1.7 km south on the Skyline Road from Highway 520. Park at
the low point in the road, off to one side. The trailhead is at the gate in the
barbed wire fence.

This hike leads to a prominent viewpoint overlooking Happy Valley, with good views west to the Livingstone Range and the High Rock Range.

Go through the gate (close it behind you), turn right (north) and follow the fence line towards the prominent hill. The grade is easy, heading up a grassy slope amid junipers, Douglas-firs and limber pines. The viewpoint is soon reached, and from it is an expansive view of the Waldron Ranch (Happy Valley). The views east are limited by the large Douglas-firs, but major ridges and ranges rise above one another in the west, with Whaleback Ridge guarding the western flank of Happy Valley. Rising above the Whaleback is the Livingstone Range, and above that the solid Continental Divide mass of the High Rock Range. On a clear day, the Elk Range is visible far to the north. On the return trip, look east to the prairie farmlands of southern Alberta.

PLAYLE CREEK

Half-day hike; moderate
Length: 6.3 km (4 mi.), Highway 22 to Skyline Road
Hiking time: 2 to 3 hours
Elevation gain: 350 m (1150 ft.)
Maximum elevation: 1660 m (5450 ft.)
Map: Maycroft 82 G/16
Access: Drive south on Highway 22 approximately 4 km past the turnoff for Highway 540. On the right side of the road opposite the trailhead, a four-wheel-drive road leads to Black Mountain. Playle Creek trail consists of two tracks cut straight up the open hillside on the left.

Although the entire route follows a cart track, the cow path in the valley is a nice alternative for part of the hike. As much of the trail is open, be prepared for the weather: carry sunscreen, a hat or rain and windproof gear. Sparse lodgepole pines and Douglas-firs in the valley and poplars at higher elevations provide the only natural protection.

The trail begins in the cow pasture across the fence beside the highway. Avoid disturbing any livestock. At the top of a rise you can see the route ahead as it leads up the creek valley to the ridge. The alternative route, the cow path in the valley, is quite pleasant with its shelter of lodgepole pines, Douglas-firs and babbling brook. Follow this or the cart track up the valley to Skyline Road on the top of the ridge. This is a good pick-up point if you have a second vehicle.

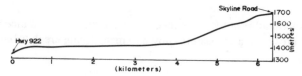

PORCUPINE RANGER STATION

Half-day hike; easy
Length: 3 km (1.9 mi.) round trip
Hiking time: 1 to 2 hours
Elevation gain: 250 m (800 ft.)
Maximum elevation: 1675 m (5500 ft.)
Map: Maycroft 82 G/16
Note: There is no water available on this hike, so carry your own.
Access: Drive south on Highway 22 to a parking area on the east side of the highway, 100 m north of the Highway 540 turnoff, or 1 km south of the Nova Gas Plant. The parking area is the former site of the Porcupine Ranger Station and some foundations remain.

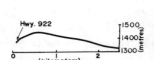

The hike ends with a pleasant view from a grass-covered hill. From the trailhead, hike the easiest route to the hilltop, following cattle and game trails when possible. From the top of the hill—or any other hill in the area—enjoy the excellent views of the surroundings. On the tops of the hills, burnt trees are evidence of a past forest fire; new growth indicates that the fire occurred at least 40 years ago.

Happy Valley, which is grazing land for the Waldron Ranch, spreads out below the west-facing viewpoints. Whaleback Ridge is west of Happy Valley, and rising above it is the Livingstone Range, and the High Rock Range beyond that. Directly to the west are the prominent forms of Tornado Mountain and Gould Dome, two peaks in the High Rock Range that rise over 2740 m. If the haze is not too heavy, you can see the Flathead Range and the Crowsnest Pass area far to the southwest.

LOWER ADAIR CREEK

Half-day hike; easy
Length: 2.3 km (1.4 mi.) to Callum Creek
Hiking time: 1 to 1½ hours (round trip)
Elevation loss: 100 m (350 ft.)
Maximum elevation: 1450 m (4800 ft.)
Map: Maycroft 82 G/16
Access: Drive Highway 22 approximately 25.5 km south from Chain Lakes Campground. The trailhead begins on the north side of the creek at a curve in the road about 1 km north of the Nova Gas Plant.

Although the trail is not well defined, the valley makes for a nice afternoon outing, as it crosses grassy pastures down to meandering creek tributaries. An option is to hike up to Whaleback Ridge using the Lower Adair Creek trailhead as a starting point.

From the trailhead, there is a view west into the valley and the Whaleback Ridge. The trail begins as a cart track that winds around a copse to a restricted access gate. Cross more pastures to another gate. The cart track becomes more overgrown and eventually fades at a hilltop. Descend the hill along cow paths to the valley bottom and Callum Creek. The crisscrossing network of tributary creeks is a favourite habitat of muskrats and beavers. Varieties of wildflowers grow on the grassy pastures and slopes; in the spring you will find crocuses, violets, old man's whiskers and shooting stars, among others. Groves of spruce trees stand on the south side of Adair Creek.

UPPER ADAIR CREEK

Half-day hike; moderate
Length: 3 km (1.8 mi.), Highway 22
to Skyline Road
Hiking time: 1 to 2 hours
Elevation gain: 270 m (900 ft.)
Maximum elevation: 1700 m (5600 ft.)
Map: Maycroft 82 G/16

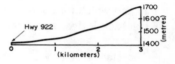

Access: Drive Highway 22 approximately 25.5 km south from Chain Lakes Campground. The trailhead begins on the north side of the creek about 1 km north of the Nova Gas Plant, on the east side of the highway.

This hike climbs to a ridge of the Porcupine Hills, where you can enjoy the fine views of Livingstone Range and the Whaleback Ridge.

The trail begins as a logging road. Keep right at several forks, always staying close to the creek. En route you will pass a large beaver dam. At a small grassy meadow where the road ends, follow a game trail alongside a dry creek bed up towards the ridge top. You may have to pick your way through heavy brush to reach the logging road. There are actually two separate roads, but they join each other at the top of the valley. Travel south on either road to the intersection of Skyline Road and Highway 540. This is a good pick-up point if you have a second vehicle. Otherwise, you will have to hike back the way you came.

For an extended hike, you can continue farther north along the ridge.

WHALEBACK RIDGE (South)

Day hike; moderate
Length: 19 km (11.4 mi.) along southern edge of ridge
Hiking time: 5 to 8 hours
Elevation gain: 600 m (1900 ft.)
Elevation loss: 570 m (1800 ft.)
Maximum elevation: 1925 m (6100 ft.)
Map: Maycroft 82 G/16
Note: Carry drinking water, as there are no creeks along the route.
Access: (North) Turn west off Highway 22, 4.2 km south of its junction with Highway 520, onto a dirt road. Proceed for 2.5 km and park at the notch in the ridge. (South) Turn west off Highway 22 immediately after crossing the Oldman River, 22.5 km north of Lundbreck. Drive 1 km along the access road and watch for a rough road coming down from the south end of Whaleback Ridge. Park here.

The stands of aspen, limber pine and lodgepole pine along Whaleback Ridge are much frequented by herds of deer and elk. The south end of the ridge features many interesting wind-sculpted rock outcrops. From the ridge crest you have extensive views of prairie, foothills and front ranges.

From the notch in the ridge (see North Access) head west towards Whaleback Ridge. Follow any one of a number of gulleys that lead up to the crest of the ridge. There are good views to the west from here. Proceed south keeping to high ground where possible and trying to avoid losses of elevation. At the 13-km mark, on the edge of the Oldman River valley, the ridge fragments into several spurs. Follow the valley that leads southeast down into Big Coulee and continue along a dirt track to the gravel access road on the north side of the Oldman River.

WHALEBACK RIDGE (North)

Day hike; moderate
Length: 15 km (9.5 mi.) along northern end of ridge
Hiking time: 5 to 6 hours
Elevation loss: 325 m (1065 ft.)
Maximum elevation: 300 m (1000 ft.)
Maps: Maycroft 82 G/16; Langford Creek 82 J/1
Note: Some bushwhacking is required along heavily forested parts of the ridge. To avoid any major bushwhacking, stay on the west side of the ridge whenever possible. A topographic map and a compass are recommended.
Access: Drive south on Highway 22 from Chain Lakes Provincial Park through the Waldron Ranch. Turn right onto a dirt road 4 km past the Claresholm junction (highways 22 and 540), follow it for approximately 2.5 km and park at the cattle guard. If you have a high-clearance vehicle, you can start the hike from the valley bottom.

The highlights of this hike along the north end of Whaleback Ridge are the frequent panoramic views in all directions. From the cattle guard, head through Waldron Ranch pastures to the valley directly west. When you reach the valley bottom, follow a prominent game trail along the edge of a small creek through a poplar forest. Although not well defined, the route is obvious and the climb to the ridge top is steady. Near the top, keep an eye out for mule deer and elk; there is a popular watering hole on the ridge. From the ridge, looking west, you can see the Livingstone Range, and the Happy Valley and Porcupine Hills are to the east. On a clear day the Crowsnest Pass area, including the Flathead Range, is visible far in the southwest.

Hike half a kilometre north along the ridge to a barbed wire fence and follow it to a treed portion of the route. Continue along the orange-flagged route and turn right onto a road at the bottom of the steep valley. When you reach a T-intersection, turn right again. After approximately 1 km turn left (east); the road takes you down a major valley towards Highway 22, passing a series of beaver ponds en route.

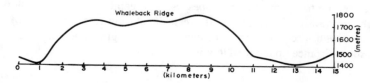

WESTRUP CREEK

Half-day hike; moderate
Length: 1.8 km (3 mi.) to summit
Hiking time: 1½ to 2½ hours
Elevation gain: 270 m (900 ft.)
Maximum elevation: 1700 m (5600 ft.)
Map: Langford Creek 82 J/1
Access: Drive about 10.5 km south on Highway 22 from Chain Lakes
Provincial Park Campground and head west on Chimney Rock Road for
approximately 3.5 km. Take the right fork for approximately 7.7 km to a
cattle guard. Park at the side of the road.

This hike does not follow Westrup Creek closely but crosses open hillsides
and climbs a rock outcrop to a small ridge. You will reach two summits, each
with panoramic views of the Porcupine Hills and the Livingstone Range.

The trail begins at the cattle guard and follows the fence left (west) into the
woods. When it begins to curve to the right, climb over the fence and head
uphill through the trees towards the open hillside. Now look for an opening in
the woods on the other side. Follow a cow path through the trees and part way
up a bald hill, then hike across and around the side of the hill. Notice an
interesting feature: the west-facing slope supports only coniferous trees,
while the drier east-facing slope supports only deciduous trees.

Continue across the open hillside, aiming for the saddle between two hills.
Do not climb too high on the hillside, as it will only result in wasted elevation
gain. On one of the well-travelled cow paths, cross the saddle to the western-
most hill. There are no defined trails here, and you must hike over open grass
slopes and through stands of poplar.

To reach the ridge, you must negotiate a section of rock outcrop, but it
does not present a major hazard. Whereas the most southerly tip of the ridge
provides the best views, it is also the least protected from the strong, constant
wind; notice the dwarfed and windblown trees. Return the way you came, or
try this pleasant alternative route: from the ridge top, head straight into the
valley, keeping to the most open slopes. Several game trails can be followed
through the valley. Across a small creek an old cut-line leads out of the
woods, through a section of marsh, and then to the gravel access road. It is
only a short distance up the road to your vehicle.

WESTRUP-LANGFORD RIDGE

Half-day hike; moderate
Length: 2 km (1 mi.) to top of ridge
Hiking time: 2 to 3 hours return
Elevation gain: 335 m (1100 ft.)
Maximum elevation: 1675 m (5500 ft.)
Map: Langford Creek 82 J/1
Access: Drive Highway 22 south from Chain Lakes Provincial Park Campground and turn right onto Chimney Rock Road. Follow it for approximately 3.5 km. At the intersection, turn right and continue for approximately 5 km. The trail, a cart track, starts at the cattle guard.

The views from the ridge of the Livingstone Range, the Porcupine Hills and Chimney Rock are well worth the 2 km of steady uphill climbing.

Ford Westrup Creek, leaving the cart track which continues to the east. Follow the fence on the left to the top of the ridge over slopes of rose bushes. (Long pants will protect your legs from the thorns.) From the ridge top, there are superb views in nearly all directions.

CHIMNEY ROCK

Day hike; moderate
Length: 6 km (3.6 mi.) to Chimney Rock
Hiking time: 2 to 4 hours
Elevation gain: 320 m (1050 ft.)
Maximum elevation: 1660 m (5450 ft.)
Map: Langford Creek 82 J/1
Note: Carry drinking water, as there are no creeks along the way.
Access: Drive Highway 22 south from Chain Lakes Provincial Park Campground for approximately 10.5 km. Turn onto Chimney Rock Road and follow it for 4.4 km. Park on the side of the road just before a cattle guard. The route leads uphill to left (south).

Those who reach the top of Chimney Rock will be well rewarded with views west to the Livingstone Range and east to the Porcupine Hills. Practise your map-reading skills on this fine panorama. There are few defined trails along the entire distance, but the route is always obvious.

From Chimney Rock Road, cross the fence to the south and aim for the hills at the north end of Whaleback Ridge. You must ford Chaffen Creek (3 m wide, calf deep) before continuing uphill beside the barbed wire fence. Stick to open terrain and make for the spine of Whaleback Ridge. Head south along the ridge, keeping to high ground. Avoid descending too far down the east side where the vegetation is heavy.

The route remains obvious along the ridge and reaches its highest elevation at the 4-km mark. It then descends to a gap below Chimney Rock. Although the most direct route to the rock is straight south through the forest, the best access is along the cut-line that leads southwest. After a short, steep climb, a well-defined trail heads south towards the rock and you will be able to see it from an open meadow. Continue on the trail as it swings around to the rear (southwest face) of Chimney Rock. Here the trail begins to fade. Continue across open grassy slopes and scramble up to the gap between two separate outcroppings. From there, turn left (north) and skirt around the rock. A final 2-m climb will take you to the summit.

Strong winds are not uncommon at the open and exposed summit. According to an Indian legend if a mounted intruder came close to Chimney Rock (known as Spiral Rock in Indian folklore) a strong gust of wind would blow him off his horse.

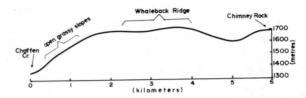

TROUT CREEK RIDGE

Day hike; easy
Length: 6 km (4 mi.) to ridge
Hiking time: 5 to 8 hours return
Elevation gain: 335 m (1100 ft.)
Maximum elevation: 1625 m (5500 ft.)
Map: Langford Creek 82 J/1
Access: Drive Highway 22 approximately 13 km south from the Chain Lakes Provincial Park Campground. The trail is a four-wheel-drive road, indicated by a gas pipeline sign on the left-hand side of the road.

This moderately graded trail takes you through mixed forest to Trout Creek Ridge and scenic views of the Livingstone Range and the Porcupine Hills.

The trail heads southeast through two pastures; in the second, look for an old corral on the right, a weather gauge on the left, and just past that on the right an overturned outhouse. The trail continues east and forks, joining again a short distance later; the trail on the left is the less steep of the two.

The road is a constant uphill from the fork, opening up in places for views to the south and west, and eventually opening up completely on Trout Creek Ridge. Turn right at a fork and climb for about 100 m. At the next fork, go left. (The Honey Coulee Valley trail is to the right.) The trail now wanders along the east side of the ridge, through a mixed forest of fir, spruce and cottonwood. You can make the short climb up on the east side of the ridge to good views of the Livingstone Range, Mount Livingstone and the Porcupine Hills. Spend some time exploring along the rose-covered hills.

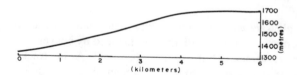

SOUTH WILLOW CREEK

Half-day hike: easy
Length: 3.6 km (2.2 mi.) round trip
Hiking time: ½ to 1½ hours
Elevation gain: none
Maximum elevation: 1250 m (4100 ft.)
Map: Langford Creek 82 J/1
Access: Drive 9.3 km south on Highway 22 from Chain Lakes Provincial Park Campground and turn left onto Riley Road, following it for 8.2 km. The trailhead is on the left-hand side soon after the blue bridge over South Willow Creek. Farm buildings are opposite the trailhead.

The trail, ideal for beginners and those with children, passes some interesting sandstone outcrops.

Around the first corner from the trailhead, go through a wooden gate into cow pastures. Be sure to close the gate securely behind you. The trail here parallels South Willow Creek with hills to the right. Except for some dwarfed and wind-blown limber pines and the sandstone outcrops, the hills are primarily bald. Soon the trail leaves the creek and continues across open pastures. Where the creek begins to flow away from the trail, notice the meander scars in the ground that mark the earlier courses of the creek.

SQUAW COULEE

Half-day hike; easy
Length: 4 km (2.5 mi.) round trip
Hiking time: 1 to 1½ hours
Elevation gain: 80 m (250 ft.)
Maximum elevation: 1360 m (4500 ft.)
Map: Langford Creek 82 J/1

Access: From Highway 22, travel east on Riley Road for approximately 4.3 km. The trailhead is on the south side of the road opposite private farm buildings, and the cart track starts between a sandstone outcrop to the east and Squaw Coulee Creek to the west. The trail is not marked on the topographic map.

This is a pleasant walk through grazing fields and provides an opportunity to observe a creek environment largely influenced by beavers.

Follow the cart track uphill to a flat, open field. As the track heads off to a stand of poplar and aspen, keep to the footpath that leads down to the creek. Several game trails wind along both sides of the creek. Beavers have thinned out the surrounding trees and their dams have created beaver ponds up and downstream.

Deer, moose and, of course, beavers, seek cover in the trees along the creek. A small tributary flows from the southeast into the coulee about 2 km from the trailhead. You have the option of turning around at the beaver ponds or exploring the valley. The trail continues through the hills to the west.

WILLOW CREEK

Day hike; easy
Length: 10 km (6.2 mi), Chain Lakes to Highway 532
Hiking time: 5 to 7 hours
Elevation gain: 150 m (500 ft.)
Maximum elevation: 1460 m (4800 ft.)
Map: Langford Creek 82 J/1
Note: Permission is required to use this route.
Access: (East) Approximately 1 km south of Chain Lakes Provincial Park Campground, turn west off Highway 22 onto a gravel road south of the Willow Creek bridge. Drive west for 2 km to cattle guard and a "private property" sign. (West) Turn south onto a gravel road 0.5 km east of Willow Creek Ranger Station.

The hike begins on a private road and leads 2 km west through aspens and poplars to an interesection. Take the right (north) fork to follow meandering Willow Creek upstream through its wide valley. The route is generally flat and easy, although you will have to cross the creek several times. (For a drier route, keep to the left at the fork.) After the second crossing, the trail leads past picturesque waterfalls where the water has shaped the sandstone rock. In the spring, yellow locoweed and blue forget-me-nots are prominent along this section of the route; notice, too, that beavers have dammed parts of the creek. After the seventh crossing, the track passes through the easternmost gates of the Bow-Crow Forest Reserve and the creek eventually reaches the main road from the Willow Creek Ranger Station. From there, you have the option of following either the creek or the road to the hike's end at Highway 532. The Willow Creek Ranger Station is 0.5 km west on Highway 532. Indian Grave Campground is 0.5 km up the access road opposite the trail's end on Highway 532.

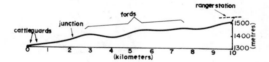

STIMSON CREEK TRIBUTARY

Half-day hike; easy
Length: 5 km (3 mi.) to lake
Hiking time: 1 to 1½ hours to lake
Elevation gain: 50 m (150 ft.)
Maximum elevation: 1540 m (5050 ft.)
Map: Stimson Creek 82 J/8
Access: Approximately 1 km north of Chain Lakes Reservoir, turn west onto Highway 532 for approximately 1 km. The trailhead, at a cart track, is on the right-hand (north) side.

Although the dense forest on much of this trail obstructs the view, the pleasant shelter is welcome on hot, sunny days. The moderately graded trail leads up the Stimson Creek tributary to a marshy lake. The trailhead is a good starting point for those wishing to climb any of the surrounding ridges; some route-finding experience is necessary.

Follow the cart track north from the highway along the east bank of a minor tributary of Stimson Creek. The route works its way through open grassland bordered by poplar forests. All along the creek, beaver dams old and new have created pools and natural bridges. After approximately 1 km, you must cross the creek on one of the dams. The trail is less well-defined on the other side, and some bushwhacking may be required to reach the marshy grassland lakeshore 1 km west. Farther west through the trees is a seismic cut-line which you can follow up to a low ridge. From the cut-line, circle back around the north side of the lake down through the trees to the original trail. This route is not well defined either, and bushwhacking is required. Wearing long pants on this hike is advisable.

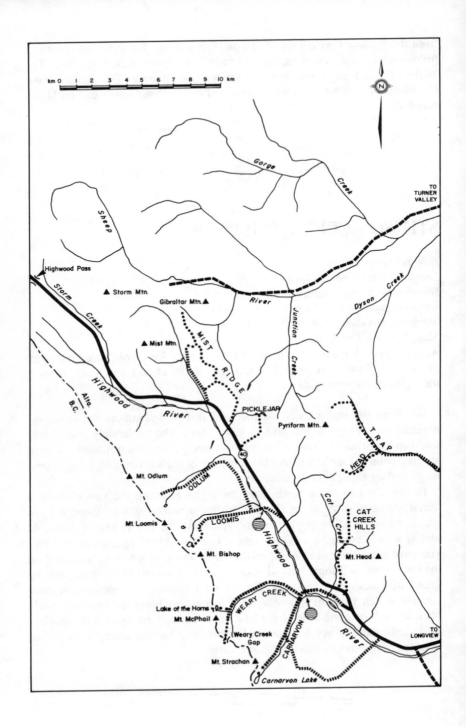

HIGHWOOD RIVER AREA

The tree line appears much higher up the hillsides of this alpine valley because of the low elevation of the valley floor, and hence the name "high wood."

The headwaters of the Highwood River are in the Misty Range to the north. Tributaries originating from the High Rock Range and joining the Highwood from the west include Odlum, Loomis, McPhail, Carnarvon and Etherington creeks. The limestone composition of many of the mountains accounts for the lack of tree cover. Since some of the limestone is oil-bearing, there are active oil and gas fields throughout the area, and many seismic roads.

Much of the forest consists of lodgepole pine, which has regenerated after thousands of hectares were burned in 1936. Many trails through the area require fords of the Highwood, thus limiting the best hiking season to late summer and early fall, when water levels are lower.

Serviced campgrounds in the area include Etherington Creek, Highwood River and Cataract Creek sites. These can be reached via Highway 541 and the Forestry Trunk Road.

Falls on Cataract Creek

ZEPHYR CREEK INDIAN PAINTINGS

Half-day hike; difficult
Length: 3.8 km (2.4 mi.) to paintings
Hiking time: 2½ to 4 hours return
Elevation gain: 152 m (500 ft.)
Maximum elevation: 1680 m (5500 ft.)
Map: Mount Head 82 J/7
Access: Drive 5.8 km east from Highwood Junction on Highway 541. Park on the shoulder and follow an ill-defined cart track 100 m to the banks of the Highwood River. The trail begins on the west side of Zephyr Creek, across the Highwood.

The highlight of this hike is a set of 300-year-old Indian paintings in a limestone canyon. They include the stick figures of a man and an unidentifiable animal, as well as a bird.

The pleasant hike leads up Zephyr Creek valley, through mixed forest with, appropriately, some Indian paintbrush blooming along the trail. Fording the Highwood River (25 m wide, thigh to waist deep, fast flowing) in the early season requires some knowledge or experience in river crossing. From the south bank of the river the route gradually heads up the Zephyr valley, passing through a stand of poplars and an open field. The route will become a single-file path. As you ascend Zephyr Creek valley, be on the lookout for the first valley along the ridge to the east. There is no clear marking on the trail to indicate the exact spot but, near this gap in the ridge, leave the main trail and head east across Zephyr valley. Cross Zephyr Creek on stepping stones.

An ill-defined trail leads along the banks of the small tributary stream in the narrow valley. Head up the stream and enter a narrow canyon. As the canyon widens, keep a sharp eye on the cliffs to the left. The red-brown petrographs are a little over a metre above ground level, and are protected from wind and rain by a rock overhang. This is an historic site, and the paintings *must not* be disturbed. A close examination of the north-facing limestone reveals the remains of other paintings that have washed away over time. Six other figures once graced the cliff, but they were destroyed in a rockfall in 1976.

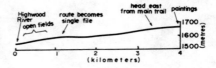

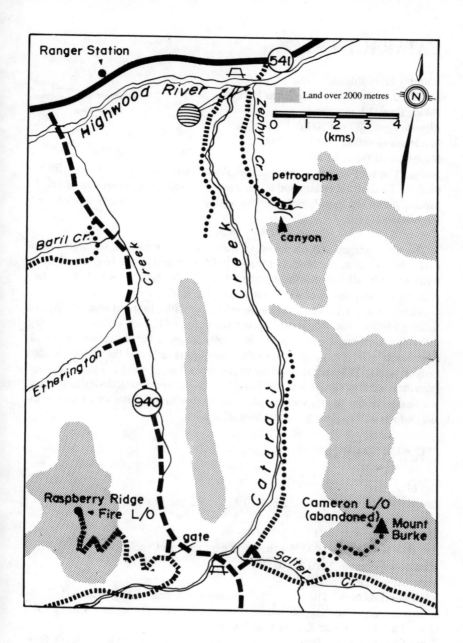

Ranger Station

Highwood River

541

Land over 2000 metres

0 1 2 3 4
(kms)

N

Zephyr Cr.

petrographs

canyon

Baril Cr.

Creek

Creek

Cataract

Etherington

940

Raspberry Ridge
Fire L/O

gate

Cameron L/O
(abandoned)
Mount
Burke

Salter Cr.

145

CATARACT CREEK

Half-day hike; difficult
Length: 2 to 3 km (1 to 2 mi.) to falls
Hiking time: 2 hours return
Elevation gain: 30 m (100 ft.)
Maximum elevation: 1525 m (5000 ft.)
Map: Mount Head 82 J/7
Access: The trail begins at the Sentinel Picnic Area on Highway 541 with a difficult ford of the Highwood River approximately 50 m upstream of its junction with Cataract Creek. Follow a rough road on the south side of the Highwood.

The deep gorges and plummeting waterfalls and rapids of Cataract Creek make this an attractive hike, but the very difficult ford of the Highwood River will dissuade all but the most ardent hikers. The hike is best left for late summer or early fall, when water levels on the river are much lower.

After the major ford of the Highwood (25 m wide, thigh to waist deep, fast flowing) follow the rough road up the west side of Cataract Creek, climbing through trembling aspen groves. It opens up on a bench above the creek where you will have good views of the numerous falls and the deeply eroded canyon walls. The trail stays close to the creek for the next 1.5 km, and then branches, leading through an enclosed forest with very limited views. It is not worth continuing unless you are planning to trek to the Cataract Creek campsite, which will require much bushwhacking.

GRASS PASS

Day hike; easy
Length: 3.2 km (2 mi.) to the pass; 10 km (6.2 mi.) to Trap Creek Road
Hiking time: 3 to 4 hours to Trap Creek Road
Elevation gain: 410 m (1350 ft.) to the pass
Elevation loss: 120 m (400 ft.) from the pass to Trap Creek Road
Maximum elevation: 1870 m (6150 ft.)
Map: Mount Head 82 J/7
Highwood Access: The trail begins on the north side of Highway 541 approximately 4 km east of Sentinel Ranger Station. The valley leading to Grass Pass is opposite Zephyr Creek valley.
Trap Creek Access: Park at the road gate inside the Forest Reserve on Trap Creek Road.

There are several options to make this a half- or full-day hike. The hike straight to the pass is shortest. For longer hikes, follow the trail up to Bull

Hills for views east to Calgary and then retrace your steps, or climb up the ridge to the west and follow it back to your car. An option for a two-car-hike is to follow Wileman Creek valley to Trap Creek Road, having cars at both ends. This can also be made a backpacking trip by continuing into Kananaskis Country from the Trap Creek–Wileman Creek intersection. All these options are easy hikes and feature good views of valleys and mountain peaks.

Beginning at Highway 541, there are two trailheads leading to the main trail, which is an abandoned exploration road. The most visible of these climbs a steep gravel bank and then follows a level bench. The other, hidden by the trees, follows part of the creek and then climbs steeply for about 0.3 km to the junction with the first trail. The main trail then begins a steady uphill climb to Grass Pass, beginning in a mixed forest of aspen and pine and large, ancient Douglas-fir. This tree cover gradually changes to aspen and poplar after 2 km, and finally to open grassland on the last stretch to the pass.

The opennesss of the pass allows clear views to the north and south, of Mount Burke down Zephyr Creek valley, Plateau Mountain and the Bull Creek Hills. Mount Head and Pyriform Mountain are among the distinguishable peaks in the Highwood Range.

For the longer options, continue down the valley towards Wileman and Trap creeks. The route is an easy stroll that begins in open grassland and gradually enters a young lodgepole pine forest with some spruce and willow beside the creek in the lower reaches.

Cross Wileman Creek on stepping stones. Two fords of Trap Creek are also required. The downstream ford follows a grass-covered, seldom-used portion of the exploration road and crosses near a campsite at the junction of the two creeks. The upstream ford adds about 1 km to the hike length, but the climb from the creek up to the trail is less arduous. The last 2 km follow another exploration road which climbs gently along the north side of Trap Creek before descending to the Forestry Reserve gate.

If a second vehicle hasn't been arranged, retrace your steps back to the Highwood Road. If you're backpacking, you can continue into Kananaskis Country by connecting with other trails along Trap Creek Road.

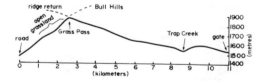

STONY CREEK RIDGE

Day hike; moderate
Length: 3.5 km (2 mi.) to ridge
Hiking time: 2 to 3 hours to ridge
Elevation gain: 700 m (2200 ft.)
Maximum elevation: 2200 m (7200 ft.)
Map: Mount Head 82 J/7
Access: The trailhead is about 150 m east of the Highwood Junction, on the north side of the Forestry Trunk Road. There is convenient parking on the highway's broad south shoulder.

This is a very worthwhile ridge walk, accessible to early-season hikers when the winter gates to upper parts of the Highwood may still be closed. From the top of the ridge the views are spectacular. The open grassland flowers include prairie crocus, Jacob's ladder, yellow violet, cinquefoil, alpine forget-me-not, shooting stars, old man's whiskers, clematis and various fleabanes. Among several options is a continued ridge walk to the northwest and a descent through Cat Creek Hills. This option is not recommended before mid-June, or you face a long trudge back along the highway.

The trail begins on the west-facing slope of Stony Creek Ridge and immediately begins to climb fairly steeply through open grassland scattered with small aspens, poplars and Englemann spruce and crisscrossed by cattle and game trails. As the trail swings right, these small paths converge on a small shoulder. From there, climb a single steep trail through more closely spaced aspen to the ridge crest; the final short stretch to the ridge is best done in several sidehill traverses. From the ridge are views of Stony Creek and Mount Head east of the Highwood River, and High Rock Range to the west. The trail along the ridge is moderately well defined and swings back and forth among rocks and into a stunted pine forest which begins with open sections and clumps of white pine, and gradually changes into continuous lodgepole and limber pine. At the 3-km mark along the ridge there is a viewpoint before a short scramble to a cairn.

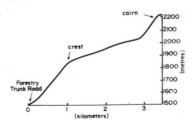

CARNARVON CREEK TO FITZSIMMONS CREEK

Day hike; difficult
Length: 16 km (10 mi.) total
Hiking time: 5 to 6 hours
Elevation gain: 25 m (80 ft.)
Elevation loss: 300 m (1000 ft.)
Maximum elevation: 1890 m (6200 ft.)
Map: Mount Head 82 J/7
Access: Drive to the Cat Creek campground, approximately 5 km north of the Highwood Junction. The trailhead is a restricted access road at the north end of the picnic site.

The two fords of the Highwood River put this hike in the difficult category. The road passes through 2.5 km of meadows dotted with aspen, and then swings west to intercept the Highwood River. Ford the river (20 m wide, thigh deep) and follow the road past a small meadow and up a hill. Take the left fork at the hill-top into the Carnarvon Creek valley. McPhail Creek forks here. After 1 km, take the left fork towards the remains of a logging camp. The trail now climbs up the ridge behind the camp and turns south to parallel the High Rock Range. You will come to many forks along this section. Always keep to the right, along the obvious, well-worn trail.

After approximately 10 km, the Carnarvon Creek trail meets the Fitzsimmons Creek trail. Turn right and head in what appears to be the wrong direction. The trail swings around south again, crosses a small stream, and soon joins the road from Baril Creek. Turn left at the next two intersections, following Fitzsimmons Creek to the Highwood River. The river must be forded before the trail end at the Fitzsimmons picnic site.

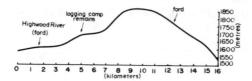

CARNARVON CREEK AND LAKE

Day hike; difficult
Length: 9 km (5.6 mi.) to Carnarvon Lake
Hiking time: 3 to 5 hours
Elevation gain: 610 m (2000 ft.)
Maximum elevation: 2200 m (7200 ft.)
Map: Mount Head 82 J/7
Access: Turn off Highway 40 into the Cat Creek campground. The trailhead is at the restricted access road at the north end of the picnic site.

Carnarvon Lake is a varied hike, combining easy initial access with the challenges of a river crossing and a short rock climb. Although neither of these is too difficult for confident hikers, clear weather and low water levels in the Highwood River still provide the best conditions for this hike to beautiful Carnarvon Lake, perched high in Gunsight Pass between Mount McLaren and Mount Strachan. Stocked with cutthroat trout, the lake is popular with local fishermen.

Hike north along the rough, four-wheel-drive road, keeping to the right to skirt the Highwood River, which is eventually forded at the 3-km mark (20 m wide, thigh deep, slow flowing). On the other side, keep left on the road to a much smaller ford of McPhail Creek. Now follow the road straight up the valley on the right bank of Carnarvon Creek. Avoid the lumber roads that branch steeply uphill to the right. Lush meadows on this stretch provide excellent campsites amidst the scattered remains of logging camps. Continue on the trail through a series of steep dips and rises. To avoid losing elevation on the final rise a half-kilometre below Gunsight Pass, move over to a trail on the right which can be seen as a lighter line on the scree slopes below the cliffs of Mount Strachan. It will lead directly to some ledges that switchback up the rock and greatly simplify the short scramble needed to finally arrive at the striking expanse of Carnarvon Lake. Here, at the northwest end of the lake, a patch of grass and scrub pines makes a good campsite.

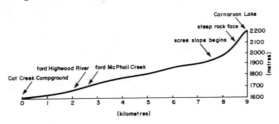

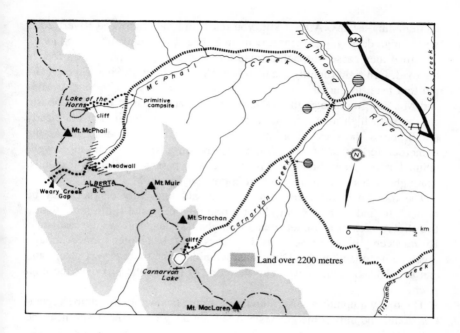

LAKE OF THE HORNS–WEARY CREEK GAP

Day hike/backpack; difficult
Length: 11.5 km (7.1 mi.) to lake; 14 km (8.7 mi.) to pass
Hiking time: 3 to 4 hours to lake, 4 to 6 hours to pass
Elevation gain: 600 m (2000 ft.)
Maximum elevation: 2200 m (7200 ft.)
Map: Mount Head 82 J/7
Access: The trailhead is at Cat Creek campground on the west side of
Highway 40, approximately 5 km north of Highwood Junction. A restricted
access road leads from the north end of the picnic area.

Lake of the Horns, or McPhail Lake as it is often called, takes its name
from the abundant horn coral fossils found near its shores. It is a large, deep
alpine lake set in a windswept rocky amphitheatre at the base of Mount
McPhail, and its exquisite blue waters and the rewarding solitude of its
setting far outweigh any discomforts involved in getting there. It is stocked
with cutthroat trout, and is popular with local anglers. Weary Creek Gap,
well within reach if you're staying in the area more than one day, was one of
the many Continental Divide passes used by the Kootenay Indians on hunting
expeditions.

Follow the restricted access road through open meadows flanked by stands of trembling aspens. After 3 km, you must ford the Highwood River (20 m wide, thigh deep, fast flowing). (Running shoes for fording are a good idea.) The road then passes through a small meadow and leads uphill. At a fork in the road, turn right (uphill) to a high bench overlooking McPhail Creek. (The left fork leads to Carnarvon Lake.) The High Rock Range, with Mounts Muir and McPhail, dominates the western horizon, and Lake of the Horns basin can be seen high along the north ridge of Mount McPhail. After a steady uphill, cross the crest of a small hill and begin a long descent. At the numerous forks that branch off the main route, always take the most well-defined road. Near McPhail Creek you will pass several beaver ponds. Throughout this section are views of impressive Mount McPhail.

The trail up to the lake from the road, although very distinct, may be difficult to find. It branches right at a primitive campsite (little more than a fire circle), crosses an outlet stream from the lake, and follows the east bank. Rising steeply in several sections, it reaches a cliff band after 1 km. Although it can be negotiated without any actual climbing, the route is very steep, and can be tricky on rainy days. The shoreline of the lake is just over the final pitch.

The rocky amphitheatre surrounding the lake lies within the alpine vegetation zone, and only some grasses and low shrubs grow in the basin, near the outlet creek at the east end. Backpackers should camp at McPhail Creek, since campsites are poor at the lake, and the environment is very fragile.

Budding paleontologists will have a field day examining the basin; fossils from an ancient seabed are plentiful in the limestone formations of Mount McPhail.

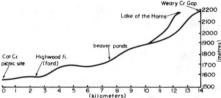

Weary Creek Gap

Instead of taking the trail up to Lake of the Horns, continue straight on the road up McPhail Creek valley. The road crosses the creek and ends just before the headwall below Weary Creek Gap. Find a route up the headwall along rough game trails. No climbing is necessary, although good scrambling ability will be required. The gap lies beyond the top of the headwall, just over a kilometre through alpine meadows. It is to the left of the low hill in the middle of the pass. Descend west from the pass to Weary Creek, a tributary of the Elk River.

An interesting option to Weary Creek Gap begins at Lake of the Horns. Although no climbing is required, this route should be undertaken only by those with mountaineering experience. Scramble up the rocky talus slopes immediately south of the outlet of the lake. From the high shoulder on Mount McPhail, find a route along the grass and scree slopes, staying above a prominent cliff band, until you emerge above the headwall to Weary Creek Gap.

CAT CREEK HILLS

Half-day hike; moderate
Length: 3.5 km (2 mi.) to top of hills
Hiking time: 2½ to 4 hours return
Elevation gain: 400 m (1375 ft.)
Maximum elevation: 1975 m (6550 ft.)
Map: Mount Head 82 J/7
Access: The trail begins on the south side of Cat Creek bridge on Highway 40. There is convenient parking on either shoulder of the road.

The trail up the Cat Creek Hills offers some great views of the High Rock Range and up the Highwood Valley. The trail mostly leads through a young pine forest. The lower portions are in aspen forest, changing to lodgepole pine and finally to mixed aspen and pine near the summit. The area is also rich in wildflowers, among them fleabane, yellow locoweed, northern butter-cup, arnica, Indian paintbrush, blue violet, shooting stars, Jacob's ladder, clematis and forget-me-nots. At the summit, there is an option to continue the ridge walk and descend the slopes to the east.

From the north side of the highway, scramble over the flood plain and along the old road base for approximately 0.5 km. Disregard the bulldozed trail which cuts back to the south, and aim for the farthest part of the bench, where a faint game and hiking trail climbs about 20 m. The trail rejoins the exploration road at the top and swings south along the edge of the bench.

When you reach the first cut-line, turn left and proceed for about 200 m before rejoining the exploration trail. Continue north on the trail, passing an abandoned mine and descending to a point near the junction of Cat Creek and a tributary from the east. Just before the creek junction, the route turns east and climbs a steep exploration trail which winds 1.5 km to the summit.

The tops of the hills afford spectacular views west to the Elk Range, the High Rock Range and Weary Gap. Views south are unobstructed along the Forestry Trunk Road towards Plateau Mountain.

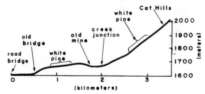

153

LOOMIS CREEK AND LAKE

Day hike/backpack; moderate to difficult
Length: 12 km (7.5 mi.) one way
Hiking time: 6 to 7 hours round trip
Elevation gain: 625 m (2050 ft.)
Maximum elevation: 2300 m (7550 ft.)
Map: Mount Head 82 J/7
Access: From the Highwood Junction, drive north on the Forestry Trunk Road (Highway 40) and park at Lineham Creek picnic area. The trail begins about 150 m north on the west side of the highway.

This is a long and straightforward but pleasant trip through mixed forest and meadows, and the last few kilometres up to a small alpine lake offer some fine viewpoints of the High Rock Range. The mountain creek and lake are named after Brig.-Gen. F. V. W. Loomis, who was with the Western Canadian Infantry in World War I.

The first kilometre of the trail leads along a gravel road to the Highwood River which you must ford (15 m wide, knee to thigh deep); this is sometimes difficult early in the season, and running shoes are recommended. On the other side of the river, follow a cart track towards the High Rock Range and Mount Loomis. After about 2 km, ford Loomis Creek. Turn left when the trail forks. As it passes through mixed forests of spruce and lodgepole pine, the trail rises gently. The small creeks are easily crossed. After about 8 km, the trail begins to fade into an overgrown and less well defined track that still follows Loomis Creek. It turns south towards Mount Bishop and begins a moderate elevation gain, and after 1 km swings back in the direction of Mount Loomis and begins a short, steep ascent. The last portion of the hike follows a rough trail up to Loomis Lake in a basin below an unnamed peak. The lake is stocked with cutthroat trout, and is a popular fishing spot.

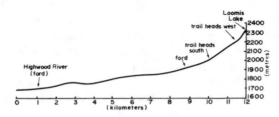

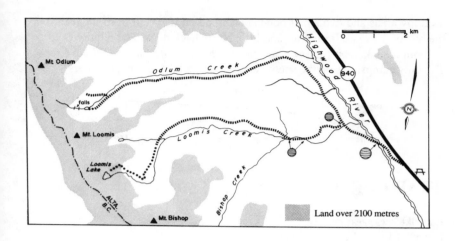

Land over 2100 metres

ODLUM CREEK

Day-hike; moderate to difficult
Length: 23 km (14 mi.) round trip
Hiking time: 6 to 7 hours
Elevation gain: 310 m (1000 ft.)
Maximum elevation: 1980 m (6500 ft.)
Map: Mount Head 82 J/7
Access: Head north on the Forestry Trunk Road (Highway 40) from the Highwood Junction. The trail starts 150 m past the Lineham Creek picnic area, on the west side of the highway.

This hike follows the Odlum Creek valley to a small lake at the foot of Mount Odlum. The road is well defined for the entire length of the hike. From the trailhead, the route leads quickly to a ford of the Highwood River (15 m wide, knee to thigh deep, fast flowing). This ford is easier later in the season when water levels are lower.

Approximately 2 km from the river, ford Loomis Creek. The trail immediately branches; take the right fork. After 3 km, the trail turns left (west) up Oldlum Creek valley. As you hike through this valley of mixed trembling aspen, lodgepole pine and Englemann spruce, keep an eye open for wildlife. This is prime habitat for all the ungulates, and moose are often seen in logged-out areas. The trail leads past an old mill site and when it eventually reaches an old bridge over Odlum Creek, there are two options. Cross the bridge and continue up a hill for half a kilometre; a further half-a-kilometre of bushwhacking is needed to reach the lakeshore.

Or, find the rough road before the bridge crossing and continue up the south side of the creek. This route leads directly to the lake, passing several swampy areas and two small ponds. The road ends 200 m from the lake, but the rest of the route is obvious and little bushwhacking will be required.

From the lake you can see a spectacular 200-m waterfall on Oldlum Creek. The only campsite is on the southwest side of the lake, among boulders.

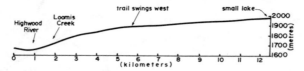

TRAP CREEK

Day hike/backpack; moderate
Length: 13 km (8 mi.) one way
Hiking time: 6 to 8 hours return
Elevation gain: 550 m (1800 ft.)
Maximum elevation: 2100 m (6900 ft.)
Map: Mount Head 82 J/7
Access: Approximately 21 km from Longview, leave the Longview-Highwood Highway (541) just before the bridge across Flat Creek. Follow the rough road from the north side of the bridge for 9 km to the restricted access gate in the Kananaskis Country Forest Management area. This road is extremely muddy and full of potholes after rain.

This is a long day hike in which the rewards come only in the final 3 km. However, if you take it as a backpacking trip, you can explore some of the interesting remote areas of Kananaskis Country. Backpackers may wish to hike into the range riders' cabin at Kilometre 7 and then use a day pack for the final 6 km to the lake. On the second day, take a short trip up Sullivan Pass, or return to explore Head Creek.

The first 5 km follow an old exploration trail through an open grassland valley abundant in wildflowers in spring and early summer.

When you reach the junction with Head Creek, you have two options. The most suitable route stays on the right (north) side of the valley and climbs steeply for about 40 m to a bench above Trap Creek. From there, it follows horse and cattle trails along the edge of the bench, and then descends to the range riders' cabin at Kilometre 7. For the alternative route, ford Trap Creek and follow the exploration trail, recrossing the creek about 500 m before the cabin.

From the cabin, the trail follows the exploration road for another 2 km, crossing Trap Creek six times. At Kilometre 9, where Trap Creek swings to the north, the exploration road continues for a short distance and ends at an unnamed creek. Follow the creek about 4 km to an unnamed lake. Between

Kilometre 9 and Kilometre 11, there are ten creek crossings as the ill-defined trail swings from side to side of the narrow V-shaped valley. Just after Kilometre 11, the trail climbs about 50 m above the creek and then climbs 225 m up the south side of the valley. Ice remains on the small lake until early July. There is a campsite on the lakeshore.

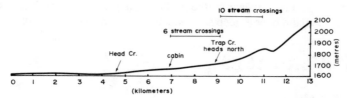

HEAD CREEK

Day hike/backpack; moderate
Length: 12 km (7.5 mi.) to ridge
Hiking time: 3 to 5 hours to alpine meadows
Elevation gain: 550 m (1800 ft.)
Maximum elevation: 2100 m (6900 ft.)
Map: Mount Head 82 J/7
Access: Approximately 21 km from Longview, leave the Longview-Highwood Highway (541) just before the bridge across Flat Creek. Follow the rough road from the north side of the bridge for about 10 km to a restricted access gate in the Forest Management area. This road is extremely muddy and full of potholes after rain.

The first half of this hike up Head Creek leads through open valley bottom typical of foothills rangeland. It features some spectacular geological formations both between Kilometres 8 and 9, and near the end of the hike at the headwall of the valley.

Follow the old road. At Kilometre 1, you can look down onto an old oil well site and some waterfalls on Trap Creek. At Kilometre 3 there is a small runoff creek, and at Kilometre 5 the road swings down to the ford of Trap Creek. Two kilometres after the ford, the road enters the narrow V-shaped valley of Head Creek.

After approximately 10 km, opposite a small creek, the trail swings sharply right and climbs gradually for 300 m, crossing a dry creek bed en

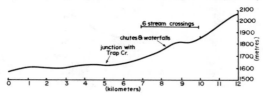

157

route. As the trail climbs more steeply along the right bank of the creek, views gradually open up to the north above the tree line. Near the 11-km mark the main trail switchbacks to the right towards the top of the ridge and a secondary trail crosses the creek over a steeply sloping meadow.

With water and shade and excellent views, this is the logical end of a day hike. Above the alpine meadow, the trail continues along the face of a steep cliff, switchbacking over a steep scree slope towards the ridge at 2400 m.

PICKLEJAR LAKES

Half-day hike; easy
Length: 3.8 km (2.3 mi,) to first lake
Hiking time: 1½ to 2 hours one way
Elevation gain: 445 m (1460 ft.)
Maximum elevation: 2125 m (7150 ft.)
Map: Mount Rae 82 J/10
Access: Access to this area is only possible after June 15, when the Forestry Trunk Road (Highway 40) has been opened. The hike begins at Lantern Creek, 2.2 km south of Picklejar Creek. Park in the parking lot south of Lantern Creek. The trailhead is about 50 m north of the twin culverts which route the creek under the road.

The Picklejar Lakes trail leads to four small subalpine lakes. The first part of the trail is indistinct and unmarked; do not be sidetracked by game trails on the south side of the creek. After about 100 m, the trail is well defined and climbs along the edge of the bench beside the creek. It climbs constantly, varying occasionally with some short dips and sharp rises. The final half-kilometre to the ridge is a steep pitch, but it is short and easily managed.

From the summit there are two possible routes down to the lakes. The easiest is to cross the pass at the lowest point and follow horse and game trails down to Picklejar Creek, then follow the creek upstream for about 0.3 km to the first lake. The alternative route follows the ridge up to a fine observation point overlooking the valley, then leads to a scree scramble down to the lakes. The short detour to the observation point is recommended; then return to the low point in the pass and descend to Picklejar Creek.

The area around the four lakes is very open, and you can spend many hours exploring and rock scrambling.

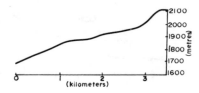

MIST CREEK–MIST RIDGE

Day hike; moderate
Length: 14 km (8.7 mi.) return
Hiking time: 5 to 7 hours return
Elevation gain: 640 m (2100 ft.)
Maximum elevation: 2395 m (7850 ft.)
Map: Mount Rae 82 J/10
Access: The trail starts from the Mist Creek picnic area on Highway 40, 21 km north of Highwood Junction and 17.5 km south of Highwood Pass. It is accessible only after June 15.

Mist Ridge has been described as one of the best and most scenic ridge walks in Kananaskis Country, and rightly so. From the top, views extend east to the Highwood Range and west to Mist and Storm mountains.

For the first 2 km the double-track trail meanders through the lower valley of Mist Creek and crosses numerous tributary streams. At about 2 km, smaller trails fork off; continue north along the main trail. For the next 2 km the main trail drops sharply to cross a creek and then begins to switchback over a grassy slope as it climbs a saddle to Mist Ridge. It then climbs gradually along the summit of Mist Ridge where there are panoramic views of the surrounding mountains and wooded valleys.

On a route that is poorly defined and difficult to follow in places, cross the west slope of Mist Ridge for 1.5 km, down a small gully and along a tributary creek to its junction with Mist Creek. The return route drops down to cross another tributary creek before rejoining the main trail some 1.5 km from the point of origin.

For one of several options on this hike, take the right fork approximately 4 km from the trailhead and climb over a pass between two peaks of roughly equal height. Now descend to Picklejar Creek and return to Highway 40.

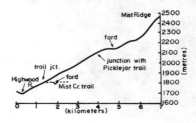

159

J. Ambrosi '81

PIKA

ADDITIONAL READING

HISTORY

Barbeau, Marius. *Indian Days on the Western Prairies*. Ottawa: National Museum of Canada, 1974.

Cousins, William J. *A History of the Crowsnest Pass*. Lethbridge: Historic Trails Society of Alberta, 1981.

Crowsnest Pass Historical Society. *Crowsnest and its People*. Coleman, AB: Crowsnest Pass Historical Society, 1979.

deSmet, Fr. Pierre-Jean. *Life, Letters and Travels of Father Pierre-Jean deSmet, S. J., 1801–1873*. New York: Harper, 1905.

Fraser, Esther. *The Canadian Rockies*. Edmonton: Hurtig, 1969.

Haines, Francis. *The Plains Indians*. New York: Crowell, 1976.

Laveille, E. *The Life of Father deSmet, S. J.* New York: Kennedy, 1915.

Major-Fregeau, Madeleine. *Overland to Oregon in 1845; Impressions of a Journey across North America by H. J. Warre*. Ottawa: Public Archives of Canada, 1976.

McCowan, Dan. *Hill-Top Tales*. Toronto: MacMillan, 1948.

McClintock, Walter. *The Old North Trail*. London: Constable, 1923.

Spry, Irene M. *The Palliser Expedition*. Toronto: MacMillan, 1963.

White, James. *Place Names in the Rocky Mountains between the 49th Parallel and the Athabaska River*. Original manuscript, 1916.

Williams, Glyndwr, ed. *London Correspondence Inward from Sir George Simpson 1841–42*. London: Hudson's Bay Record Society, 1973.

NATURAL HISTORY

Hardy, W. G., ed. *Alberta, A Natural History*. Edmonton: Hurtig, 1967.

Geology

Beaty, Chester B. *The Landscapes of Southern Alberta*. Lethbridge: University of Lethbridge, 1975.

Vegetation

Cormack, R. G. H. *Wild Flowers of Alberta*. Edmonton: Dept. of Industry and Development, 1977.

Hosie, R. C. *Native Trees of Canada*. 8th ed. Don Mills: Hosie & Whiteside, 1979.

Porsild, A. E. *Rocky Mountain Wild Flowers*. Ottawa: National Museums of Canada, 1979.

Watts, Tom. *Rocky Mountain Tree Finder*. Berkeley, CA: Nature Study, 1972.

Animals and Birds

Godfrey, W. Earl. *The Birds of Canada*. Ottawa: National Museum of Canada, 1966.

Mays, Buddy. *Guide to Western Wildlife*. San Francisco: Chronicle, 1977.

Rand, A. L. *Mammals of the Eastern Rockies and Western Plains of Canada*. Ottawa: National Museum of Canada, 1948.

Salt, Walter R. *The Birds of Alberta*. rev. ed. Edmonton: Hurtig, 1976.

Note: Both the Audubon Society and Houghton Mifflin (Peterson Field Guide Series) publish a fine series of pocket field guides on a wide range of natural subjects.

HOARY MARMOT

Fording Daisy Creek

Index of Hikes